ONE BOY'S BOSTON

1887-1901

ONE BOY'S
BOSTON
1887–1901

SAMUEL ELIOT MORISON

with a Foreword by
EDWARD WEEKS

NORTHEASTERN UNIVERSITY PRESS
Boston

Northeastern University Press edition 1983
Copyright © 1962 by Samuel Eliot Morison
Reprinted by permission of Houghton Mifflin Company

Library of Congress Cataloging in Publication Data

Morison, Samuel Eliot, 1887–1976.
One boy's Boston, 1887–1901.

Reprint. Originally published : Boston :
Houghton Miffllin, 1962. With new introd.
1. Morison, Samuel Eliot, 1887–1976.   2. Boston
(Mass.) — Social life and customs.   3. Historians—
United States — Biography. I. Title.
E175.5.M66A36 1983   974.4'61041'0924 [B]   83–19296
ISBN 0–930350–49–9 (alk. paper)

The paper in this book meets the guidelines for permanence
and durability of the Committee on Production Guidelines
for Book Longevity of the Council on Library Resources.

Manufactured in the United States of America
88   87   86   85   5   4   3   2

To

PRISCILLA BARTON MORISON

latest and most beautiful of the chatelaines

of 44 Brimmer Street

PREFACE

IN THIS little book I am merely jotting
down memories and impressions of
childhood and boyhood in Boston, sixty-
odd years ago; and of some of the people
who passed through, or influenced, my
young life.

S. E. MORISON

44 Brimmer Street
Boston, February 1962

FOREWORD

WHAT I find so endearing about this little classic is that while the "begats" in the opening pages are of relevance only to the families concerned, Samuel Eliot Morison's recollection of his Boston boyhood in the closing years of the nineteenth century preserves the inquisitiveness of youth and the idiosyncracy of one's elders in such a delightful American contrast. He was born on July 9, 1887, and was destined to live his remarkably productive years at 44 Brimmer Street, the elastic house of red brick built on the bank of the Charles River by his grandfather, Samuel Eliot. I say "elastic" because in the 1890s it sheltered his two grandparents on the second floor, Sam, his younger brother, and their parents on the third, and five servants on the fourth. And on festive occasions, such as the dance for Sally Norton, it encompassed forty-three debutantes, their fifty-five escorts, and the orchestra.

Sam's grandfather, Samuel Eliot, was a scholar, cousin of President Eliot of Harvard, and himself president of Trinity College, Hartford, until he was eased out by a faculty intrigue. Subsequently he was appointed superintendent of the Boston schools, and with a broadmindedness inherited by his grandson, had a bowdlerized edition of *The Arabian*

Nights prepared for school use. The charge of "corrupting our youth with licentious tales" compelled him to retire to his library, an invaluable room to Sam the Younger which, with his mementos of Columbus and of our naval operations in World War II, came to be the most picturesque private library in Boston.

It was the horse that gave 44 Brimmer Street its special redolence. "I began riding at the age of five," he writes, "and ours was the horsey end of town," occupied by livery stables and many private ones, blacksmiths, coachmen, carriage builders, and a regiment of well-bred horses. When the snow was deep there was coasting down Beacon Hill and "punging" on the runners of a sleigh; in summer the air had a "rich equine flavor, especially on days when the stablemen were pitching manure into the market gardeners' trucks." There was no keeping the flies out and Sam's grandmother offered him a cent for every fly he could kill indoors. When the bill for one day rose to $1.12, the tariff was cut. Later, he adds this Pickwickian touch: "after becoming Professor Hart's assistant at Harvard I would combine business with pleasure by riding my gray gelding 'Blanco' to Cambridge, tying him to a tree in the Yard, and loading the saddlebags with students' papers that had to be corrected."

The one big "hate" of Sam's boyhood was *Little Lord Fauntleroy*. "Thanks to Mrs. Burnett's namby-pamby juvenile hero, boys were dressed in velvet with lace collars and red stockings; and if their hair had any curl in it, forced to wear 'love locks.' I was one of these victims." His grandparents rescued him when they took him on a visit to

Admiral and Mrs. Sampson at the Charlestown Navy Yard
in the fall of 1899. The Admiral sent him on board the old
receiving ship USS *Wabash* where he was measured by the
naval tailor for a sailor suit with bell-bottomed trousers,
never suspecting "that little Sammy ... would one day be
said Navy's historian."

All his life Sam loved the theater and he and his cousin
"Mac" would pool their resources to attend a Saturday
matinee. Once they were dead broke when Weber and
Fields came to town with Lillian Russell and De Wolfe
Hopper in the cast, and "in desperation we persuaded my
grandmother to take us. The good lady, to whom Weber
and Fields had been represented as comic-opera impresarios of a high order, knew she had been 'had,' but took it
like a very good sport — '*Very* vulgar, but I suppose you boys
just *had* to see Lillian Russell!'"

In those placid days before the motorcar, a boy could
roam downtown Boston and the waterfront, take the penny
ferry across the harbor and ask to be allowed aboard a
Cunard liner or a full-rigged ship in the lumber trade.
Nights on Brimmer Street were peaceful until the cater-
wauling began and was finally hushed by a neighbor who
hurled Fourth of July torpedoes at the love-makers. Sam's
"informal alarm clock" sounded at eight when his grandfather began playing hymns on the upright piano in the
library. It was a gracious way to grow up.

EDWARD WEEKS

CONTENTS

ILLUSTRATIONS

THE ELIOTS AND THE OTISES

ONE autumn day in 1887, Dr. Charles Montraville Green, "with his little round hat and his walking stick and his beard of pubic hair" (as the famous "Ballad of Chambers Street" describes him), was walking along Brimmer Street, at the foot of Beacon Hill in Boston. As he approached No. 44, his astonished gaze beheld a baby carriage, unattended, bouncing down the stone steps. Upon hitting the sidewalk it pitchpoled, hurling the contents — one mattress, one pillow and one baby — into Brimmer Street. By a strange quirk of fate the mattress landed first, with baby on top, and the pillow on top of him. Dr. Green rushed forward, expecting to administer first aid to the howling infant, but found him unhurt, and identified him as Samuel Eliot Morison, whom he had brought into the world at the same house on the previous 9th of July.

What had happened was simply this: nurse Lizzie Doyle, pausing at the top of the steps to gossip with the parlormaid, momentarily released the perambulator's handle. Since no harm ensued, Lizzie was forgiven, and she continued as my nurse long enough to be remembered with deep affection.

Number 44 Brimmer Street, where I was born and still live, had been built by my maternal grandparents, the Samuel

Eliots, during the winter of 1869–70, which they spent in
Paris. They started home just before the Franco-Prussian
War broke, taking passage in the Cunard side-wheeler *Scotia*.
She was commanded by a bearded captain who always made
a point of kissing the first-class lady passengers goodbye at the
end of the voyage. Before reaching this osculatory terminus at
Boston, *Scotia* called at Halifax and anchored in the stream.
The gentleman passengers, who included James Bryce and
A. V. Dicey, were mad to get at the Halifax newspapers and
read news of the war; but the captain insisted on every news-
paper being deposited in his cabin, and reading them himself,
before he would allow any to go out.

Samuel Eliot, born in Boston in 1822, was a grandson of
the Samuel Eliot who founded a professorship of Greek at
Harvard, after accumulating a fortune in the mercantile
business, most of which was dissipated in the next generation.
His daughters managed to keep their shares, which enabled
their respective husbands to "live like gentlemen" while engaged in unremunerative professions; but son Samuel Atkins
(father of President Charles W. Eliot) lost his in the panic of
1857, and our share went down the drain even earlier. My
great-grandfather, William Havard Eliot, who lived at No.
56 Beacon Street, invested most of his patrimony in shares
of the Tremont House, on the corner of Beacon and Tremont Streets, which for many years was accounted the best
hotel in the United States. Upon his untimely death, in 1830,
his widow followed the bad advice of an executor in throw-
ing these shares on the market at a fraction of their cost, and
became a comparatively poor woman. This meant that my
grandfather Samuel Eliot, after graduating from Harvard

first in the Class of 1839 (Edward Everett Hale being second, and my other grandfather, Nathaniel Holmes Morison, third) had to go to work, and that his younger brother never did enter college.

Samuel Eliot prepared (the old word was "fitted") boys for college for several years. He then attained a chair of history at Trinity College, Hartford, and became president of the College in 1860. During a winter's trip to Europe, for his wife's health, he was eased out of that position owing to a faculty intrigue, and the Eliots returned to Boston to live. There my grandfather, who was wholly devoid of false pride, accepted the position of first headmaster of the Girls' High School, which he raised to such a standard of excellence that it was attended by many young girls of my mother's social set. He was then appointed Superintendent of Schools of Boston for one term, but failed to be reappointed because he published a very bowdlerized edition of *The Arabian Nights* for school use. A rival who wanted the job twisted this into "Corrupting our Youth with the Licentious Tales of an Oriental Despotism," and Dr. Eliot returned to private life. He accepted this humorously and philosophically — as he did all losses and crosses in life; an attitude doubtless made easier because his wife had brought enough money into the family for them to live comfortably without the aid of a salary.

She was Emily Marshall Otis, daughter of the one-time celebrated beauty Emily Marshall, and of William Foster Otis, son of Harrison Gray Otis the Boston grandee. The Otises were genial, worldly and luxurious in their tastes; the Eliots were frugal and ascetic, dedicated to literature and other good works. Although Harrison Gray Otis had been a leader in Federalist politics and Senator from Massachusetts, he was better known for his wit, charm and hospitality. The three mansions that he built in succession, 141 Cambridge Street opposite the Old West Church, 85 Mt. Vernon Street, and 45 Beacon Street, the last two designed by Bulfinch, are still standing; and he bought a large farmhouse at Watertown, provided it with a Bulfinch oval dining room, and used it as a country estate. It is now the Oakley Country Club.

My great-grandmother, Emily Marshall Otis, died in childbirth in 1836. Her two little girls, Emily my grandmother, Mary who became Mrs. Alexander H. Stevens, and George (a childhood friend of Henry Adams), then lived in their grandfather Otis's mansion at 45 Beacon Street, where they were brought up under the care of a widowed aunt. My grandmother assured me that there was no plumbing of any description in that great house; all the water had to be brought in from a well in the yard. She, Mary and George were marched to the Tremont House once a week for a tub bath.

Samuel Eliot, a poor but handsome and popular young man, courted Emily Otis. Her father preserved, and I now have, this little note in which he formally asked for her hand:

June 22, 1852

My dear Sir,

I have asked your daughter Emily to love me, and she has given her consent. I come, now, to ask for yours.

I do it reverently. For I can feel how much I am asking of you.

But I do it earnestly, with my whole heart. Emily says she thinks I can make her happy. If I did not hope that I could, I would not ask her of you. But I have told her, as plainly as I know how, that I am not, and that I shall not be, a rich man. Years ago, as I have said to her, I chose a calling, which, the more conscientiously it is pursued, the less abundant is it in pecuniary returns. Notwithstanding, Emily believes she will be contented. I believe she will.

I make my request to you, my dear Sir, with the deepest feeling. It seems to me, as if God had offered before me the prospect of a great blessing. To you I turn, trusting, entreating, that it may be confirmed.

Pray let me have your answer as soon as you can.

With my true regard,
I am yours,
SAM¹ ELIOT

Emily Marshall Eliot, as she now became, inherited the Otis charm and sociability. I have never seen a more gracious smile on any woman. She had a genius for making people of any age feel at home; although, as far as small children were concerned, this gift was assisted by her unique institution, the "present drawer." In her downtown shopping expeditions she kept an eye open for things that little boys and girls might like. These were wrapped up, marked with their contents, and placed in two bureau drawers in her bedroom, one for boys and one for girls. Every child who came to the house was led to this bureau and allowed to make his choice. That was what did the trick — you could pick out what you wanted.

Grandfather did not much care for evening parties, but Grandmother loved them, and even, on occasion, went without him. Once, when hoop skirts were still in fashion, she returned to 44 Brimmer Street alone after a dinner, dismissed the carriage, found she had no latch key, and could awaken nobody with the doorbell. So, she hung the hoop skirt on the back fence, climbed over, and got in by the dining room window, fortunately unlatched. At that juncture a constable came along, saw the hoop skirt hanging in a horrible attitude on the fence, assumed that there had been foul play, blew his whistle and summoned reinforcements; so that before long everyone in the house, and the neighborhood, too, was awake. Explanations were given, beer was produced for the cops, and all ended in laughter, as things generally did in that household.

Another story about her, much relished in the Boston of my childhood, was "How Emily Eliot put the President out of his Private Car." Proceeding to New York from Hartford, she entered the nearest parlor car at the railroad station and sat down near the door. Presently there entered at the other end a number of gentlemen smoking long black cigars. My grandmother summoned the conductor and ordered him to "request those gentlemen to stop smoking." The conductor somewhat hesitatingly executed this command; the gentlemen, instead of putting out their cigars, promptly removed themselves to another car. Presently there appeared before my grandmother her friend the Hon. Hamilton Fish, Secretary of State. He was laughing so hard he could barely say:

"Mrs. Eliot, do you know what you have done?"

"No!"

"You have put President Grant and some of his cabinet out of his private car!"

"What? I never guessed that that bearded gentleman with the long cigar was the President."

"Why, Mrs. Eliot, didn't you know he was taking this train?"

"Well, it's true that I heard people on the platform saying 'Mr. President this,' and 'Mr. President that,' but you know, Sam had been President of Trinity College, so I thought nothing of it! Pray make my apologies to *The* President."

Grant took the incident pleasantly, and when told by Mr. Fish the identity of the lady, remarked, "Nobody but a granddaughter of Harrison Gray Otis could have done that without being offensive."

The Eliots went in for education, literature and scholarship. President Eliot and Charles Eliot Norton were my grandfather's first cousins, and he served on the board of almost every major charitable institution in and around Boston. But the Otises, like W. S. Gilbert's

> . . . *House of Peers, throughout the war,*
> *Did nothing in particular.*
> *And did it very well.*

Mother was very fond of her cousins Harry, Bertie and Willy Otis, gay dogs and benevolently delightful to small boys like myself. Among the parties described in my grandmother's notebooks, the only one that I attended and can still remember was a luncheon in 1897 for Mr. and Mrs. Herbert Otis, memorable for the wit of "Cousin Bertie."

A typical Otis story about Bertie's brother Willy, one of my father's Harvard classmates, I heard much later; and as he left no descendants there is no reason why it cannot be told now.

Willy was married to a Miss Root. They had no children, but Willy kept a mistress in a house on Shawmut Avenue, and had two or three children by her. There he was known as Mr. Jones, a clerk in the Customs House, whose duties required long, unexplained absences. During the summer the Otises kept a cottage at Nahant. Willy used to take the morning boat to Boston, visit the downtown office where he had nothing to do but clip coupons, lunch at his club, spend the afternoon at the Shawmut Avenue love nest, and catch the 5 P.M. boat back to Nahant. Willy's wife adored him; but her mother hated him, put detectives on his trail, found out about his double life, and confronted her daughter with the evidence. She refused to believe a word of it. So Mamma decided to get the evidence for herself. She hired a cab, waited outside the Shawmut Avenue house, and when Willy came down the front steps, kissing his children goodbye, she flounced out, crying "Now William, you rascal I've caught you! And I am going straight home to tell your poor deceived wife."

Willy, apparently unperturbed, bowed deeply. "Madam, you are mistaken; I am Mr. Henry Jones of the United States Customs Service" — handing her the visiting card especially engraved for such emergencies. "Nonsense!" said the old lady, tearing the card in two, "You are wicked Willy Otis, my son-in-law, and I am going right down to Nahant to tell your poor trusting wife about your despicable conduct." Snorting loudly, she got into the cab, and drove slowly off.

Willy did some quick thinking. He sent one little boy to the nearest Western Union office with a telegram to a livery stable at Lynn, near the depot, ordering his favorite fast trotter to be harnessed to a buggy, and with driver to meet him on the arrival of the 4:30 train. Figuring that his mother-in-law, with her tired old cab horse, would miss that train, and guessing that upon arrival at Lynn she would await the hourly horse bus to Nahant, he sent a second boy to fetch a cab which stood on a nearby corner to serve sporting gents, and offered the cabby ten dollars to catch the 4:30. The cab galloped down Charles and Cambridge Streets, passing Mrs. Root's slow-moving vehicle with ease, and Willy was just in time to swing onto the rear car of the 4:30 as it started. At Lynn the horse and buggy were ready. The driver drove it over Lynn Beach as though competing in a trotting race. At the foot of the hill that leads to Nahant village, Willy left his buggy, tipped the driver heavily, instructing him to walk the horse all the way back to Lynn; and himself walked up the hill. There he was greeted by his trusting wife on the front porch of the Otis cottage.

"Why Willy dear, why are you home so early?"

"Darling, I had such a hot, tired day at the office, that I took an early train home, and I'm quite exhausted!"

"You poor dear, go right upstairs and get into bed, and I'll bring you some cool lemonade."

"Thank you, darling, I believe I will" — and did.

Willy's calculations were correct. Mamma missed the 4:30 train, and when the 5:00 arrived at Lynn, waited for the next slow bus. A good hour after Willy's arrival she bustled up the steps, announcing "Now my dear, will you believe me? This very afternoon I caught your wicked husband on Shawmut Avenue, surrounded by his little bastards!"

"Why, Mamma, why will you say such things about dear

Willy? The poor boy came home early from the office and is now upstairs asleep in bed!"

Mrs. Root flung up her hands, exclaiming, "Well, I give up!"

She made no further efforts to disillusion her daughter, and the marriage lasted happily to Willy's death in 1893.

Great-uncle Alexander H. Stevens, who married my grandmother's sister Mary, was a New York banker. They had a large, jolly family, with whom my mother was always exchanging visits. One of their daughters was the beautiful Emily Ladenburg, mother of May (Mrs. Preston) Davie; their son Eben was the father of my dear friend and shipmate, William D. Stevens. Uncle Alec told me with evident astonishment that my grandfather, in spite of being a scholar, was a good man of business; and that must have been true, because he managed my grandmother's share of the Otis fortune — which had been split six or seven ways — so that they were able to build 44 Brimmer Street. Its location, too, was determined by old Harrison Gray Otis. He had been one of the farseeing Bostonians who developed the Copley pasture on Beacon Hill into a residential district. That is why the main streets were given good Federalist names, such as Mt. Vernon, Pinckney and Revere. When the Back Bay was partially filled in ("with discarded hoop skirts and tomato cans," as the saying was), my grandmother's share was the area over the flats west of Charles Street, north of Chestnut and south of Mt. Vernon. So my grandparents built a house on the corner of Brimmer and Mt. Vernon Streets for themselves, and Nos. 4, 6, and 8 Otis Place, and 156, 158 and 160 Mt. Vernon Street as an investment.

Clouds descended momentarily over this pleasant household when Uncle Willy Eliot, my mother's only brother, died in 1874. His was a lingering death, from tuberculosis of the hip, caused (it was said) by a fall when sliding down the banisters at 44 Brimmer. He took his final examinations for his Harvard degree in bed, watched Class Day from a window of Harvard Hall, but wasted away and died before the year's end. Willy was a young man of promise, destined for the Church, and my grandfather never ceased to mourn his loss. He was terribly offended because, some twenty years after their son's death, my grandmother forgot the date and accepted a dinner invitation.

With a young girl in the house life went on, and in due course "Emmy" Eliot, at the age of eighteen, came out in society. At that time Boston debutantes numbered only about twenty-five damsels, whose parents knew one another; and the purpose of a debut was supposed to be to introduce them to their elders. But Harvard College, as before and since, seemed created for the debutantes' special amusement. My mother's coming-out party was held in 44 Brimmer Street. Linen cloths were tacked over the carpets, which in those days extended from wall to wall, a small orchestra was had in, and an elaborate supper served at about 2 A.M. Special friends and beaux were urged to stay after three, when the guests began to thin out, and at five a breakfast was served to them.

The amount of food consumed at these parties seems monumental. In my grandmother's notebook of parties at 44 Brimmer Street, I find an account of one given for Sally Norton, a daughter of Charles Eliot Norton, who was coming

out. Forty-three girls and fifty-five men assembled in this
small town house to honor Sally. They danced to a three-
piece orchestra; and at supper consumed, according to the
hostess's record, five quarts of creamed oysters, a salad built
around twenty-five pounds of lobster, a twelve-pound filet of
beef, two twelve-pound turkeys, eleven chickens, eight dozen
rolls, six dozen individual ices, and four quarts of plain ices.
Yet the alcoholic consumption was limited to a case of
champagne and a few bottles of sauterne and claret.

At family dinners the usual wine was sherry or madeira.
My grandfather had a fine cellar of madeira, part of a cargo
that came over in the barque *Nautilus* in 1852. News having
reached Boston of a famine raging in Madeira, a number of
gentlemen, who had been almost weaned on madeira wine,
chartered this vessel, filled her with provisions of every kind,
and dispatched her to the hungry island. The grateful Ma-
deirans filled her hold with their choicest wines of ancient
vintage, and returned her to Boston, where the subscribers
divided the cargo. A wonderful instance of bread cast on the
waters returning after many days. Grandfather set aside for
me a case of the *Nautilus* madeira, which lasted long enough
to be featured at dinners of Sohier Welch's Club des Arts
Gastronomiques; and Grandfather Morison, equally gener-
ous and farsighted, set aside for his son, who left it to me, a
case of William Ziegler's "Gamecock" Maryland Rye, dis-
tilled in 1857 and 1860.

2

ENTER JOHN HOLMES MORISON

E MMY ELIOT, after surviving several Boston social seasons and rejecting sundry swains, was finally persuaded to bestow her affections on John Holmes Morison, son of her father's classmate. He had the advantage of having been born and raised in Baltimore, where his father was Provost of the Peabody Institute. This gave him more courtly manners than the general run of Boston young men, who called him "The Maryland Squire," or simply "The Squire." John and Emily were married in 1886 at Trinity Church. "The Squire" was regarded as a rising young lawyer; but as he was not earning enough fees even to pay office rent, he and my mother were persuaded without much difficulty to live at 44 Brimmer Street, where the third floor became known jocosely as the "Morison Flat." This arrangement was so mutually agreeable that it continued indefinitely. When my birth began to be predictable, Dr. Green announced that a new bathroom must be built for "the flat." At that time there was only one complete bathroom in the house, off the Eliots' bedroom. The third floor, and the fourth where the servants' bedrooms were, had only a slop closet for emptying the jars, and a cold-water faucet. But the new bathroom was built, and my grandfather is said to have "groaned" over the expense — one hundred dollars.

Naturally I do not remember the episode with which this book opens. My first memory is of Nahant, "Cold Roast Boston," where my parents took a cottage for two or three summers. The picture engraved on my infantile mind was that of my nurse at the time, "Nana" Coombs, who was pinch-hitting for Lizzie Doyle. A pyramidical elderly woman in bonnet and shawl, she was being literally boosted up the steps of the Lynn bus by two men. "Nana" Coombs was a Dickens character, a regular Mrs. Gamp. My father, eager to improve her mind, started her off on *The Vicar of Wakefield*. After a few attempts at perusal she returned it with the comment "Never knew such a born fool in all my days as that there Moses selling a colt for a gross of green spectacles. If *that's* all Sir Walter Scott can write about, I don't want no more of them Waverley novels!"

The first time I ever noticed a date (the merchandise in which destiny required me to deal), was that of 1891, at the head of an ornate Louis Prang calendar. Having a retired grandfather, whom I adored, as head of the household, I was put to my books early, at the age of three; and before the fifth year came around, he started me on French. Grandfather believed firmly in the old-fashioned method of learning by rote. Finding no existing French books suitable, he procured a blank notebook and wrote out the paradigms in his neat hand, thus:

Present	*Past*	*Future*
j'aime	j'aimais	j'aimerai
tu aimes	tu aimais	tu aimeras
etc.	etc.	etc.

For a long time I thought that "j'aime" was the way Frenchmen of my generation said "I love," and that "j'aimais" was how they used to say it; but how Grandpa figured out that they were going to say "j'aimerai" in the future I found difficult to comprehend.

Nevertheless, it was wonderful to have a loving grandfather always on tap to answer questions, and in a library — the same as my library today — which included no end of illustrated books fascinating to a small boy. I pored over Dr. Elisha Kent Kane's *Arctic Explorations,* which is now beginning to be appreciated as one of the best American books of the century. Cousin Lily Cleveland gave me for Christmas 1894 Molly Elliot Seawell's *Decatur and Somers,* which kindled my interest in naval history. For that I bless Cousin Lily, albeit she was a Victorian of Victorians. She always dressed her hair like the picture of Princess Victoria being informed she was Queen; and she worked through all the English poets in her father's library, blacking out the lines in Byron and Shelley which she considered erotic.

3

THE HOUSEHOLD
AT 44 BRIMMER STREET

O UR HOUSEHOLD, in the 1890's, was large and happy. In the house where Priscilla and I live today with one cook-housekeeper, there were then eleven people — the two Eliots, the Morison parents, myself, younger brother, and our nurse; a lady's maid, a cook, a parlormaid-waitress, and a chambermaid. The last, for fifty years or more, was Lizzie Turner. She came to us when my mother was a young girl from the Berkshires, where she had been trained in domestic service by the Sedgwicks; and she died at 44 Brimmer Street in the 1920's. Lizzie resembled those family slaves whom one encounters in the Greek dramatists, or in Racine; always faithful and loyal, always jealous for the family's reputation, pregnant with sound advice and old saws. When I went away to school she tried to press dollar bills into my hand, and admonished me to be a credit to the family. She expressed herself freely on the character of our visitors; one whom she described as an "old rip" was thenceforth regarded with suspicion. When Uncle George came to dinner some ten years after graduating from college, and my father proposed to break out brandy for him, Lizzie said, "You shouldn't give such strong liquor to so young a man!" When I built a camp on Mt. Desert Island, she gave me the wherewithal to build a rowing skiff, which I named *Lizzie Turner* after her; and the skiff, though somewhat "nail-sick," is still doing duty today.

Lizzie, though of Yankee stock, was a Roman Catholic, which enabled her to dominate a kitchen where the cook, the waitress and the chambermaid were always Irish Catholics. Irish born they mostly were, too; girls of character, whom we loved and they us, although they generally stayed only long enough to find a Boston Irish husband. Our big basement kitchen, with its coal range, was an informal clubhouse for the neighborhood servants and their friends, and a favorite place for my friends and myself to make popcorn on a winter afternoon. My nurse and the maids had numerous relations scattered along Charles Street or on the back side of Beacon Hill; and when they were supposed to be walking me in the Public Garden, I was apt to be conducted into one of these fascinating one-room tenements, where the coal stove was the center of life. The mothers greeted me as "darlint," and gave me a share of whatever was cooking, while the children stared at me suspiciously. These nurses gave the "well-bred" children of my generation an intimate touch with a life of which the carefully groomed and mamma-raised suburban kids of today are unhappily ignorant. The nurses not only showed us how the poor lived, but imparted folklore and wisdom that cannot be got from books.

One of these bits of folklore, illustrated by the nursery rhyme about little boys being made of "snips and snails and puppy-dogs' tails," related to the dire consequences of evil doing. If a small boy were too bad, God in desperation would change him into a *girl!* This I so firmly believed that, when a lady with a distinct mustache passed us in the street, I asked my nurse whether she had not originally been a bad boy, whose metamorphosis was incomplete.

If children of the poor (and why not "poor," instead of that idiotic phrase "underprivileged"?) stared at little Sammy suspiciously, it was because he wore long yellow curls and was dressed to suit. This brings up the one big hate of my childhood, the infamous creation of Frances Hodgson Burnett. Her *Little Lord Fauntleroy,* which appeared the year before I was born, had a disastrous effect on many fond mammas of that era; the more so on mine, as she had hoped for a girl. Thanks to Mrs. Burnett's namby-pamby juvenile hero, boys were dressed in velvet with lace collars and red stockings; and if their hair had any curl in it, forced to wear "love locks." I was one of these victims. The nurse used to make up my blond hair into golden ringlets every morning, turning them with her spittle around a sort of minor police-man's baton, and I was not allowed to have them shorn until the age of seven. About one boy in ten of that era, subjected to this indignity, suffered gibes, insults and hair-pullings innumerable from his more fortunate fellows; and I was that one in my infant schools. We victims would all have cheerfully contributed our pocket money to have Mrs. Burnett and her odious creation boiled in oil.

The only member of the domestic staff still unaccounted for is the lady's maid. She was always French or Swiss-French, so that my grandmother and mother could keep up their proficiency in that language. Her room on the top floor contained a sewing machine and had a grate, where a coal fire was kept burning in winter; on rainy or snowy afternoons this room was the meeting place for nurses and children, we being allowed to run the sewing machine and share the cocoa made over a gas ring. The entire house was lighted by gas; electricity was not introduced until about 1910, one of the reasons being that the maids were afraid of it. Rightly so, too; for if you touched one of the all-metal light switches of that era when standing in a tin bathtub, you short-circuited the works and were lucky not to be electrocuted.

The gaslights were in chandeliers hanging from the ceilings of the dining room and library, and in wall brackets in the other rooms. Every evening the parlormaid went around with one of those long-handled gadgets such as are now used for lighting altar candles, turning on the chandeliers' gas keys and lighting the burners with a loud pop. In the library, a flexible tube connected the chandelier with a table gas lamp, around which my grandparents read in the evening. The Morisons had their own sitting room in "the flat" and used a tall brass kerosene lamp to read by, instead of the gas. Many of the gas pipes and burners leaked slightly, so that there was always a faint odor of illuminating gas in the house. Gas, too, were all the street lamps; every day at dusk the lamplighter came around, with a long pole that had some sort of spark at the tip, to turn them on, but the city turned them off automatically at dawn.

Besides the servants who lived in, there were others who came in — Mrs. Bens the laundress, Mary Ann Todd, a Scotswoman who helped with the sewing and did plain dressmaking, John Foley, who started as the corner cabman and became neighborhood choreman and factotum. He shined the men's shoes, stoked the furnace, carried wood and coal upstairs for the open fireplaces and grates, set out the ash cans and swill buckets. John, too, was a useful bridge between my sheltered life and reality. I remember his saying, "We all voted against Henry Cabot Lodge because he tried to restrict immigration and we wanted to bring all our friends over from Ireland; but I tell you, Sammy, we wouldn't do so today. Go out on the Common some Sunday afternoon and listen to them furrin' anarchists and socialists! I tell you, Sammy, if them fellers get on top they'll make the French Revolution look like a church picnic." If John had lived to 1918 I would have congratulated him.

The street, too, was full of characters. There was an old colored man with a wooden leg, a veteran of the Civil War, who stumped over to the Public Garden every sunny day, sat on a bench and beamed at the children. There was a seedy character, said to be a Harvard graduate, who apparently made his living picking over trash cans; when engaged in that not very intellectual occupation he would doff a battered straw hat and address one in the most cultured accent: "Going abroad this summer, Mrs. Eliot?" or "Did you attend Mrs. Endicott's ball last night?" Once he reproved me severely because I answered him "Yeah!" instead of "Yes"; said I simply *couldn't* be a Boston boy to talk that way.

Odenwald the cobbler, in front of his shop on Chestnut Street (between Charles and River Streets), circa 1900.

Chestnut Street, Boston, circa 1890. Joe Pink's harness shop, where horse deals were made around a pot-bellied stove, is on the left.

4

A HORSEY NEIGHBORHOOD

THE HORSE, which entered this story as the saviour of
Cousin Willy Otis's marriage, was my companion from
earliest childhood; I began riding at the age of five, and ours
was the horsey end of town. Almost the entire square between
the backs of Beacon, River and Mt. Vernon Streets, and the
river, was occupied by stables big and little — livery stables,
which let out "sea-going" hacks and coupés; boarding and
baiting stables, where gentlemen who drove in from the suburbs behind fast trotters left their rigs during the day; club
stables where individuals could board one or two horses;
dozens of private stables. Chestnut Street between Charles
and the river was called "Horse-Chestnut Street" in derision.
Near the corner of River Street was Joe Pink's harness shop,
redolent of saddlery, where horse tack was made and re-
paired, and the fraternity made horse deals around the pot-
bellied stove. On Lime Street, there were at least two blacksmith shops, where the cheerful ringing of hammer on anvil
could be heard from 7 A.M. to late afternoon. There was
Chauncy Thomas's carriage factory on lower Chestnut Street,
where beautiful sleighs, victorias, broughams and other horse-
drawn vehicles were built; Frederic J. Fisher, the famous
body designer for automobiles, there had his training. All

this afforded abundant opportunities for an inquiring small boy to advance his education by picking up learned opinions from stablemen, coachmen and blacksmiths on how to select and breed a horse, on equine maladies, proper horseshoeing and the like; information which the jolly Irishmen who practiced these arts were only too ready to impart. Horse lore was often expressed in rhymes, such as:

> *One white stocking, try him,*
> *Two white stockings, buy him;*
> *Three white stockings and a white nose,*
> *Strip off his skin and feed him to the crows.*

My descendants will find it hard to believe that I once kept a horse at the Beacon Club Stable for daily rides to Jamaica Pond or beyond, or for driving a girl to the Country Club on Sundays; and that even after becoming Professor Hart's assistant at Harvard I would combine business with pleasure by riding my gray gelding "Blanco" to Cambridge, tying him to a tree in the Yard, and loading the saddlebags with students' papers that had to be corrected.

One center of interest for horse enthusiasts was Fire Engine Company Number 10, in its present location at the corner of Mt. Vernon and River Streets. No. 10 kept four magnificent dapple-gray horses, which the firemen exercised between fires, riding them bareback up and down the street. A wonderful spectacle was touched off by the fire alarm. Doors to the horse stalls opened automatically; each horse went to its place at engine or hose wagon; the harness, even the collars, dropped into place on their backs and necks; firemen slid down poles, buckled the tackle, lit the fire under the brightly polished brass boiler; and within sixty seconds of the first bell, engine and hose went roaring out into the street, the horses at full gallop. Lucky was the boy who happened to be on hand, to catch a ride to the fire on the tail of the hose wagon.

It was a great mortification to the neighborhood that No. 10's apparatus happened to be helping at a distant fire when the greatest fire in Brimmer Street history broke out,[1] in Brown's stable between Chestnut and Byron Streets. This occurred after Brown had compromised with the automobile to the extent of letting his stable be used as a garage and filling station. The fire quickly spread to the gasoline tank. I heard the explosion, looked out, and saw a great flame shooting across Brimmer Street, menacing the wooden stable on the site of the Burdett Business College. That was saved, but Brown's burned to the ground. It was replaced by the brick Brimmer Garage, where George Giffen and his merry men now give that "service with a smile" which is often promised but seldom found.

This horsey atmosphere, delicious to the rising generation, was less favorably savored by our elders. It gave the air a rich equine flavor, especially on days when the stablemen were pitching manure into the market gardeners' trucks which came to take it away. Swarms of flies penetrated 44 Brimmer Street in spite of the screens, pirouetting gaily around the chandeliers when not attempting to share our meals. My grandmother, in desperation, offered me a cent for every fly

---

[1] No. 44, already built when Boston's Great Fire of 1872 broke out, was saved by my grandmother's having the roof covered with wet blankets, which prevented the flying embers from catching.

I could kill indoors, and for several days I was in the money; but after I had incautiously run up the score to $1.12 in one day, the tariff came down sharply. Sticky flypaper was then substituted for Sammy and his swatter, to the discomfiture of family cats. Reader, if you have never seen a lively kitten mixing it up with a sheet of "Tanglefoot" flypaper, you have really missed something in life.

All this depressed real estate and made Brimmer Street unfashionable; that made no difference to our family, but the maids used to say to me, "Master Sammy, do persuade your grandpa to move to a swell neighborhood, like Commonwealt' Avenoo!" The revenge of time has reversed these values. With the passing of the horse, stables and blacksmith shops were pulled down or converted to dwellings, and a syndicate of enterprising young men, led by Matthew Hale, put up the neat, neo-Georgian brick houses that now line lower Brimmer Street, Lime Street and Charles River Square. The smells departed with the horse; but so, alas, did the rather sporty and raffish atmosphere of the neighborhood. It has become eminently respectable, and property there or on Beacon Hill is at a premium, over that of the once proud Back Bay.

Horse-drawn, too, was our public transportation until I was six or seven years old. A much-quoted ditty was the satirical poem of a Bostonian expatriate:

Oh! to be born in Boston, in the chill of a winter day,
To the family tree of a social grandee, and the tap of a pap-frappé;
With a cousin at every corner, and on every street an aunt;
To be known "who you are" on the Little Green Car,
And your family seat at Nahant.

With your "old man" strong in the market, and in mourning "Mamma
so missed";
A hunter or two, and a Trinity pew, and a vanishing visiting list.
Ah yes, to be born in Boston, introduced by a spectacled stork;
In our great social spawn 'tis the place to be born —
But, ye gods, let me live in New York!

This Little Green Car was the horse-drawn car which
started somewhere on Massachusetts Avenue, trotted down
Marlborough Street, skirted the Public Garden to Charles,
passed along Cambridge to Staniford, and descended the West
End hill to the North Station. Lying in bed at night I could
hear it tinkling past Brimmer and Beacon, then again past
Charles and Mt. Vernon; hear the one bell that signaled the
horses to stop, and two bells to start. The Little Green Car
stopped anywhere on signal, not only at corners. The con-
ductors knew everyone along the route, and the residents knew
their names, and even those of the horses. A lady would put
a small tot on board and say to the conductor, "Mr. Kelly,
would you please see that little Mary gets off at her Aunt
Anna's — No. 152 you know?" and Mr. Kelly would, and did.

I do not wish to sentimentalize over the horse age. Motor
transport is responsible for many ills, but it certainly has
saved the world an enormous amount of equine and even
human misery. Not every man and boy who handled a horse
knew how to do it properly. Privately owned saddle horses,
horsecar horses, and the sleek, well-fed animals in private
stables were well treated, but the workhorses were commonly
overworked, underfed, and subject to senseless beatings by
ignorant or brutal drivers. A frequent sight in winter was
that of a horse falling down in harness, through slipping or

sheer exhaustion; and I recall one occasion when a driver
was whipping an animal prostrate in the snow to make him
get up. My father intervened, stopped the cruelty, and
showed the man how to unbuckle the harness and free the
horse so he could get up. My mother tried to intercede with
an express company to stop one of its drivers from galloping
his horse past our house every evening, bringing him to the
nearby stable all hot and sweaty, so that the man could go off
duty a few minutes earlier.

So, too, with the cab and hack drivers. I used to wonder
why they were so gruff; it was partly no doubt that they got
no tips, since that was not a tipping age — tipping was supposed to be decadent, servile, a European relic. Mostly, however, the cabbies' gruffness was caused by their patrons' lack
of consideration, keeping them waiting for hours on a cold
night while they dallied at a party. It was a frequent sight
to see hack drivers walking up and down slapping their sides
with their arms to restore circulation, while the horses stood
shivering under a blanket. Once, walking home on a night
when the temperature was around zero, I passed a house
where several hacks were waiting for dinner guests to get
ready to leave; one of the drivers, looking toward the front
door, exclaimed, "If those goddam rich bastards don't come
out quick, I'm going in there to tell them to hell with them
and they can walk home; I'm not going to stay here and freeze
to death." So, I'm not shedding any tears over the passing
of the horse from our cities, where, with few exceptions, he
lived a short and miserable life, tended and driven by overworked and underpaid men.

Waiting for work on the new subway, Charles Street corner, March 1895. The construction of Park Street Station began that month and was completed in 1897. It was the first subway station in the country.

A traffic jam on Tremont Street opposite the Boston Museum in 1896, as horses jostle with trolleys for control of the city streets.

 5

TROLLEY CARS, CABS AND BICYCLES

OWING TO the opposition of Marlborough Street residents to trolley cars, the Little Green Car, and its partner the Blue Back Bay Car, which left Marlborough at Dartmouth and proceeded down Boylston to Tremont, hung on to about 1902, long after the rest of the West End Street Railway (parent of the M.T.A.) had been electrified. These early trolleys added to the gaiety of the scene by their varied colors. Roxbury cars were green; those that served Dorchester, a rich royal purple; Cambridge cars (appropriately) were crimson; those to South Boston (inappropriately), scarlet; Brookline cars pale blue; Brighton's sober brown; Somerville and Charlestown cars a defiant maroon. There was also a one-track yellow "Belt Line" car which careered along Charles Street and around downtown Boston to Roxbury Crossing, then down Columbus Avenue to Charles Street again. Small children passengers were torn between looking out of the window or spelling out the fascinating advertisements. We marveled at the literary and allusive ability of the De Long Company, which announced:

> *The cable-cars may lose their grip*
> *The horse-cars sway and bump;*
> *But one there is that never slips,*

Its name is on the million lips
That murmur, See That Hump!
The De Long Hook and Eye

We admired the typographical ingenuity of the laundry which advertised

F AMOUS   C OLLARS
  LEXIBLE   ANNOT
  INISH   RACK

And our mouths watered at Deerfoot Farm's assurance, built around a picture of an attractive piglet, that its sausages were "Made of Little Pigs and Choice Spices."

The ironical thing is that these primitive trolley cars, with open platforms, afforded better public transportation than one can get in Boston today. Along Charles Street we had the choice of five different lines: the downtown Belt Line, Cambridge, City Point, Clarendon Hill, and the North Station. Today you either wait twenty minutes for a bus that takes you only to Bowdoin Square, or walk to Charles station and cross the traffic circle by a precarious sort of suspension bridge.

In the 1890's there were no automobiles in Boston, except a few experimental machines which were always breaking down. These, when proceeding jerkily, with alarming pops and sputters, gave the more spirited horses an irresistible desire to leap into the Public Garden or climb somebody's front steps. About 1901 there appeared on the street, briefly, a fleet of closed electric taxicabs, so clumsy and with such huge rubber tires that they were nicknamed "elephants on dumbbells." Before that, the principal means of public transportation not on rails were the herdic and the horse cab. The former, peculiar to Boston, was a miniature omnibus on two wheels, in which four big or six small passengers, entering from the rear, could sit facing each other, paying twenty-five cents a head. The herdic seems to have been designed as a vehicular hair shirt; a ride in one over the cobblestones of downtown Boston jolted the very teeth out of you. The more respectable horse cabs cost fifty cents per person from downtown up to Dartmouth Street; seventy-five cents or a dollar if the destination were further west. Frugal Bostonians were said to locate below Dartmouth Street in order to save the difference; but they did not patronize the cabs much anyway — you either kept horses (our family did not) or used the streetcars. My cousin Isabel Morison, after marrying Frank Grinnell, announced "I'm going to bring my daughter up so she can take a cab without feeling like a fallen woman."

The advent of the "safety" bicycle, about 1893, was a boon to all young people, and a partial release from dependence on the horse. Everyone under fifty learned to ride, either at Colonel Pope's bicycle rink on Columbus Avenue or on a quiet side street like ours. Every spring evening there would be fifty to a hundred couples passing our door, the girl learning how to ride, and the young man running along and holding on to the handlebar or saddle to prevent her crashing. My parents and I went in for bicycling with enthusiasm. The best make then, the Columbia, cost $100, but there were many competitors; my first, a Lovell Diamond, a wonderful Christmas present from the entire family, cost about $30.

Strangely enough, our neighborhood is quieter at night

nowadays than in the 1890's. The routine, as I remember it, in spring and fall, was this. From dusk to about 10 P.M., the street was filled with young people learning to ride the bicycle, and resounded with tinklings, crashes, squeals and giggles. Around 11 P.M. came dog-walking. Everyone about us seemed to own a dog, which had to be taken out before bedtime. Since there was no traffic that a healthy dog couldn't easily dodge, the pooches were left loose; this led to healthy competition at the lampposts, and gave owners a chance to exchange gossip. After it was thought that the pets had done enough, there was a great whistling, and cries of "Here, Rover!" "Come here, Jack!" and the like to separate them from their tail-wagging friends.

By the time dogs were safely housed, cats began their nocturnal concert. Across Lime Street from our back yard, at the site of No. 38, was a vacant lot, shaded by large poplar trees and enclosed by a picket fence. Since it was overlooked by no windows from which water could be discharged, this was an ideal spot for feline courtship, which, as everyone knows, is exceedingly noisy. After this had continued for some time one would hear window sashes across the street thrown up, and shouts of "S-S-S-Scat!" These were completely ignored by the cats; but Charles Eliot Ware, who lived at No. 49 Brimmer, now went into action. He had a method of breaking up the Tom Loves Tabby routine which was worse than the music. Having laid in a stock of mammoth Fourth of July torpedoes, he hurled them one after another into the cats' pleasure park; and the explosions (which awakened every neighbor who had dozed off during the caterwaulings) were followed by frantic feline scrambling over back fences, and complete silence.

But not for long. In those days milk, at eight cents a quart, was delivered in the early morning hours, from one-horse wagons, in gallon tin cans. Competition was so keen that some six different milkmen had routes which took them along Brimmer Street at hours between midnight and dawn. Each visitation meant a clop-clop-clop of horses' hooves, rattling and creaking of the wagon, and the clanging of cans against each other and the bricks. And, if two or more milkmen met, loud conversation and laughter. After the last milkwagon departed, around 4 A.M., the citizenry could sleep peacefully until seven when the blacksmith shops opened for business, and loud, prolonged tootings of whistles on the factories across the river announced that the workingman's day had begun.

My informal alarm clock sounded at eight, when my grandfather began playing hymns on his upright piano in the library, and the two canary birds joined in, cacophonously. There was just time for a boy to tumble out of bed, dress, give face and hair a "lick and a promise," and get down to eight-fifteen breakfast. Grandfather, who sat at the table's end, under a dropsical rubber plant that partially concealed the window, got there first to look at the not very startling headlines in the *Boston Daily Advertiser;* but he put it aside when my grandmother entered, and gallantly pulled out her chair. She sat at the inboard end of the table, smiling sweetly, wearing a lace cap and presiding over a huge silver coffee and tea set. Breakfast, as I remember, was innocent of grapefruit, orange, or other vitamins — a name still to be coined. Baked apples and a course of hot cereal were followed by great platters of bacon or ham and eggs, or just plain eggs with fish. When Uncle Alec or Cousin Eben

Stevens came from New York to stay, the fish had to be Boston scrod; and there usually ensued a learned argument between the New Yorkers and the Bostonians as to exactly what was a scrod? What the Manhattan theory was, I forget — probably something with tomatoes — but my grandfather stoutly maintained that a scrod was, or should be, a small codfish that had been split and slack-salted the night before.

A snowy ride on Beacon Street. The Public Garden is to the left and the entrance to Brimmer Street is on the right.

Photograph by T. E. Marr, courtesy of the Print Department, Boston Public Library

Winter traffic on Beacon Street, February 1901.

❧ 6 ❧

SLEIGHS, PUNGS AND SKATES

I N THAT horse era snow was a blessing rather than a curse. Every vehicle went on runners. The hacks were replaced by "boobys,"[1] covered sleighs with coachlike bodies, cozily lined with red plush or silk. Wealthy people had open two-horse sleighs with fur-clad coachmen and footmen on the box. Suburban sports drove in town in one-horse "cutters," racing each other along Beacon Street. Trucks and delivery wagons became one- and two-horse "pungs," a Novanglicism which the Oxford Dictionary of American English tells me is remotely derived from "toboggan." Pungs as well as sleighs were the vehicles of the small-boy sport of punging, indulged in during school recesses or on winter afternoons. You ran after the sleigh, placed your feet on a runner and held on, enjoying the thrill of what seemed superlatively rapid transit. Boys who failed to catch the sleigh shouted "Cut, cut behind!" which was an invitation to the coachman or driver to wrap his whip about you; but they seldom did. Beacon Street, during recess from Mr. Noble's school, was the scene of rapid

[1] This word, short for "booby-hutch" or "booby-hut," is a Novanglicism of colonial days. The derivation is unknown; my guess is that it was suggested by the covered sleigh's resemblance to the booby hatch — the companionway all in one piece, like a yacht's "dog house," which was used on quarterdecks of merchantmen.

punging to and fro. The high, ever memorable moment came when Dave Webster, later a distinguished physicist, caught an open hearse, and grinned at us defiantly over the coffin.

Coasting on the Common or Beacon Hill had been going on since colonial days. A story of the American Revolution that impressed my infantile mind was that of the Boston boys appealing to General Haldimand to restore their immemorial privilege of coasting on the Common, which the "lobster-backs" had temporarily forbidden. Girls coasted there, too; my mother told me how she had a sled named "General McClellan" (all sleds were named in those days) which was much admired, but the time came when other children pointed at it and hooted, so she ran home crying and had a piece of carpet tacked over the then disreputable name.

The ex-McClellan was still up in the attic during my childhood; but I disdained it as a girl's sled, on which one coasted sitting down. The Flexible Flyer had not yet been invented; boys' sleds were merely pieces of board with two six-inch wide, steel-shod runners, and a handhold in each runner, forward. At the top of the hill you grasped the sled by these handholds, ran furiously, and then hurled yourself and sled on the snow, to coast down "belly-bump." The Common hill was steeper then, before fill from the first subway was dumped on its slopes, and it was poor coasting indeed that did not take you and your sled all the way to the fence on Charles Street. Two boys' sleds connected by swivels with a long board made what was called a "double-runner"; this was the ancestor of the Swiss toboggan, for which international teams compete on the famous Cresta Run at St. Moritz. Our toboggan was the original American Indian kind, and was used for coasting down very steep slopes in the country, or on specially built and iced runs, of which there were several in the Boston suburbs. The ski was unknown in New England until the twentieth century.

Beacon Hill streets were also favorite places for coasting; sometimes a boy with a flag would be posted on Charles Street to warn against an approaching vehicle. One contemporary won fame by steering his sled under a trolley car, between the forward and rear trucks. When Uncle Frank Morison decided to move from unfashionable Chestnut Street to swell Commonwealth Avenue, his son James MacGregor, known as "Mac," burst into tears, crying "There are ten good reasons not to leave Chestnut Street." When invited to name them, Mac said, "The first is the coasting — and that goes for the other nine!"

During school recesses, when the ice began to break up, we enjoyed the sport of "tiddledewinks," or "running tiddely," on the Public Garden pond. This meant crossing the pond by running over floating ice cakes and jumping from one to another. At such times, the Public Garden rang with cries of "Hey, tiddely!" as the boys dared each other; and hardly a day passed wherein one hero did not fall in, to be sent home, wet through and shivering, or to be dried out by kind Mrs. Trower, the school housekeeper. Our elders never seemed to mind these escapades; there was a saying that no Boston boy was a real boy until he had fallen into the Frog or the Garden pond, but that none ever drowned there.

Rarely, very rarely, skating was allowed on the Back Bay,

through which the salt tides surged until about 1910, when the Charles River dam was installed and the Embankment, site of Storrow Drive, was built. Until then, Mt. Vernon Street ended in an iron fence parallel to the back yards of Otis Place. The wall under the fence was lined with smelt fishermen at the right season. From my grandfather's library I could watch tugs and barges plying the river to and from the Watertown arsenal, and even an occasional schooner sailing along. Uncle George Morison opposed the fill-in. "Why?" said I. "Because it will prevent Joe Lee" (who lived on the water side of Brimmer Street) "from keeping a rowboat on davits." "Well," said I, "I have often rowed by the Lee's back yard, and I never saw any boat on davits." "That's true," said Uncle George. "He always meant to, never did, but now he can't!"

Until around the age of twelve to fourteen, when organized sports began, boys of that era had a lot of free time. My pals and I did a good deal of roaming through downtown Boston and along the waterfront. We would take the penny ferry to East Boston, call at a wharf where a Cunarder or Leyland liner was lying, and ask to be allowed on board. On one memorable occasion we climbed all over the full-rigged, three-skysail yard ship *Aryan,* then in the lumber trade to the river Plate. Sometimes we would catch an early afternoon train to Kendal Green, where I boarded my fox terrier Jack with an elderly lady who loved dogs. Jack was exiled to the country after it was found impossible to prevent him from rolling in manure, or jumping on beds. One of the smooth-haired variety, he became so cold and shivery one winter night that I took him to bed with me. Mother, arriving a little late to perform the nightly ritual of "hearing Sammy's prayers," found me already asleep, with Jack's furry head next mine, and his body under the bedclothes. That marked the end of Jack's city residence. But his exile to Kendal Green gave me and my friends a good excuse to go there afternoons or weekends, to give Jack a walk and ride Frank Byrne's pony.

Small boys did a good deal of calling at one another's houses to play with each other's toys. In the photograph of my grandfather in the library you may observe, at lower left, part of a circular track; that was the "elevated railroad," a present from New York, around which a little train ran by clockwork. It fascinated all my friends, as elevated railroads were the latest thing in rapid transit and Boston had none. Sam Vaughan owned a beautiful miniature locomotive that used real steam, generated by an alcohol lamp under the boiler; and at one time he had a small printing press, upon which we printed our names on cards. Incidentally, do my readers remember what a thrill it was first to read one's name in print? That I suppose, is part of the childish egocentric world that is so charmingly described by A. A. Milne in *When We Were Very Young.* In the big town houses of our period there was always a room set aside for nursery or children's play room; the Pickman brothers had a sort of gymnasium at the top of their parents' house near Noble's school, where we wrestled, boxed and tried gymnastic stunts.

҈ 7 ҈

THE SHOPS ON CHARLES STREET

CHARLES STREET between Beacon and Cambridge was a much cozier street in my childhood than today, since it has been widened. The shops were largely confined to the blocks between Beacon and Mt. Vernon Street, and there were few of them. Clough & Shackley, Summers, and Welch's fish market are the only ones that have changed neither character nor location since 1900. There was not a single antique shop, and no florist nearer than a little basement one around the corner on Beacon Street. De Luca's fruit store was there, but under its original proprietors, Solari & Porcella, on whom my grandfather used to try his Italian with indifferent success since he spoke the language of Dante and they were Sicilians. In the next block, on the west side, was a hardware store kept by Charles Pierce, which seemed to stock everything under the sun. On the east side there was Chapman's fish market and Chater's Bakery, which had a lunch counter, the only semblance of a restaurant in the entire district. There you could buy a bowl of soup or a ham sandwich for five cents — chicken sandwiches ten cents. On the southeast corner of Mt. Vernon was Greer's Variety Store, where you could plunge your arm into a big goldfish bowl of green pickles in vinegar and select your favorite, price one cent. Across the street was Murphy's Grocery. And I cannot forget John Cotter's saloon between Mt. Vernon and Chestnut. "Honest John," or one of his barkeeps, could be seen every fair morning sprinkling the sidewalk in front of his establishment with water in which heeltaps from the previous day's consumption were dissolved. The resulting odor was highly inviting to passing gentlemen with alcoholic tendencies. The real saloon center, however, was around Cambridge and Charles Streets. Cambridge was then dry, and the old West Boston bridge (precursor of the Longfellow) was the only horsecar route to the Center of Learning. So gentlemen stopped off at the transfer point, where the traffic circle now is, to take one or two "for the road."

Marcus the tailor in those days plied his useful calling in a basement shop on Beacon Hill. Another old-timer, still alive though retired and succeeded by Frank Longo, was Jake Greenberg, whose shoe repair shop was next John Cotter's saloon. Perhaps as a tribute to the cultural prestige of the neighborhood, Jake disdained the usual notice "Shine, 5¢," and had painted an elaborate announcement, as follows:

Pedal Integuments
Artistically Illuminated
For The Infinitesimal Remuneration of
5 Cents Per Operation

It may be wondered how ladies did their ordering for a large household like ours before the days of the telephone; and we never had a telephone before the new century. Grandmother, with apron on, descended to the kitchen every morning to confer with the cook. An hour or so later appeared the "man from Pierce's" to jot down grocery orders in a notebook, for delivery later in the day. Staples such as flour, sugar, potatoes and apples were bought by the barrel; all the bread and cake we used, except for parties, was baked in the house. The week's needs for meat, poultry, eggs and fish were figured out in advance and ordered by my grandfather personally at Faneuil Hall or Quincy Market on Saturday mornings. It was a treat for me to accompany him, to note the respect with which he was greeted by the jolly red-cheeked marketmen (who wore straw hats winter or summer), and to receive a fig or an orange as a present. If these logistic calculations did not turn out correctly, I was sent on an errand to procure what was necessary. Most of my pocket money was made running errands, telling Hanson's stable that Mrs. Eliot wanted a hack that afternoon, and delivering written invitations to parties.

Up the hill at Pinckney and West Cedar Streets there was Alfred Brigham's market, which the genial Joe Sheenan, who came there to work as a boy, is operating today. On Charles Street, between Mt. Vernon and Pinckney, was the shop of Mahoney, Gentlemen's Tailor, which was considered much too expensive for the likes of me. After happily graduating from the Little Lord Fauntleroy age, and little boys' sailor suits, we wore three-piece woolen suits, costing about $10 or $12, which were purchased from piled-up heaps of ready-made clothing at Shuman's or Macullar Parker's on Washington Street. Until the age of fourteen or fifteen boys wore knee pants, black cotton stockings and high black boots, which were partly laced over hooks. Baggy knickerbockers and "golf stockings" with folded-over tops came in around 1899.

Shirt collars were always stiffly starched and detachable. For headgear, we wore a round woolen cap like a sailor's watch cap, or a so-called Eton cap that covered only the back of the head. Some boys, subjected to a more manly but no less irritating literary influence than Mrs. Burnett's, were put into Eton collars and jackets for parties, or for Sunday church; but most of us on such occasions wore a dark blue suit and a derby hat. Boys were put into long, horribly scratchy woolen underwear in the fall, and not allowed to wear cotton shorts and shirts until April. They played games in these clothes, with a sweater substituted for the jacket, and seldom had a chance to bathe afterwards. The heavy underwear was considered necessary because houses and schools were far less heated than today. At 44 Brimmer Street the hot-air furnace only reached the second floor, and not all of that; the bedrooms had grates where anthracite coal fires were lighted only in cold spells.

On the street boys were supposed to wear gloves, or at least carry them in their hands, like their elders. I remember Grandfather looking out of the window and, seeing his classmate Edward Everett Hale gloveless, remarking "There goes Ned Hale, as usual without gloves — can't he learn that a gentleman *always* wears gloves?" It was commonly said of the eminent author of *The Man Without a Country* that if he were dining out he wore his tails and white tie all day, so as to avoid the trouble of changing. Grandfather, for all his neatness in dress, was unconventional in many ways. For instance, if the traffic were not too dense, he always walked in the middle of the street, since the brick sidewalks of Beacon Hill hurt his feet. This drew jocular or snide remarks from passing wagons, and occasioned no small mortification to me as a small boy; but Grandfather didn't care; he just beamed and waved at the person and trudged ahead.

Photograph by N. L. Stebbins, courtesy of the Society for the Preservation of New England Antiquities

Downtown Boston, circa 1900. The Old Corner Bookstore, at the intersection of School and Washington Streets, is still standing.

Courtesy of the Metropolitan District Commission, Boston

Strolling down the Esplanade in style.

The three Sams—Morison, Vaughan, and Eliot—circa 1901.

The author, aged twelve, in his new jacket.

PRIVATE SCHOOLS

A LL THE schools I attended were private. The first, which I entered at the age of five, was kept in the front parlor of the Lyman house on Beacon Street, now the Women's City Club; the next, by a Miss Hudson, on Chestnut Street, one door up from Charles. One of my fellow students there was Amos Chapman, son of the local fishmonger; another, Francis Yeats-Brown of future *Bengal Lancer* fame, son of the British consul. Francis looked, dressed and acted like a little prince. When asked his opinion of the teacher, he replied in a very superior voice, "I find Miss Hudson rather fatiguing!" But he had such imagination as to be a leader among the small boys of the neighborhood. At one time he thought up a scheme of building a sort of steam caravan to travel about the country on missions of knight-errantry. As much as $3.50 was collected from his friends for this admirable object when he made the mistake of "touching" the Consul for a tenner, and was forced to refund everything; much to the dismay of his contributors, who really believed that it would work.

Next, I attended a really progressive school for those days, the Shaw School at 5 Marlborough Street, with well-trained, sympathetic women teachers — the Misses Woodward, Hazard and Peirce, one to each grade. They dramatized the most ordinary subjects for us, and were so advanced as to have a class in carpentry, which they called "sloyd." There I made some of the friends who lasted me through life — Bill Homans, Philip Weld, Sam Eliot and Sam Vaughan — the last two and I were thick as thieves and even had our photo taken together, the "three Sams." From 5 Marlborough most of us passed into Noble and Greenough's, then at 97 Beacon Street; a school for boys only.

In the first decade of this century there were at least four private schools for boys in the Back Bay or Beacon Hill — Hopkinson's, known as "Hoppy's," on Mt. Vernon Street; Noble's; Stone's in the same block; and Volkmann's, on Newbury Street, just above Massachusetts Avenue. The Volkmann building is still there, but Mr. Volkmann suffered from the detestation of things German in World War I and had to close. Hoppy's and Stone's have also passed away, but Noble and Greenough's took a new lease on life by becoming a country day school at Dedham.

Mr. George Washington Copp Noble, Harvard 1858, had been head of this school since founding it in the sixties. He was greatly beloved, but the boys took advantage of his age and deafness by extensive prompting — at one time Bill Minot was doing the Greek lessons for our entire class. Mr. Noble's son-in-law and partner, James J. Greenough, known as "Black Jim" from his somber coloring and stern expression, was an excellent Latin scholar, but very stern; my father once had to remonstrate with him for setting sixty lines of the *Iliad* daily. The other masters were gentlemen, scholars and good teachers; I remember with particular gratitude

Mr. Francis Kershaw, who introduced us to good English literature, and drilled us in acting scenes from *A Midsummer Night's Dream*. The course was strictly classical and college-preparatory; seven years of Latin, four of Greek (or, if your parents preferred, as mine fortunately did not, German); and for the rest, French, Mathematics, English Literature and Composition, Ancient and English History; and for the last two years, Chemistry and Physics. Of this school, attended for four years before going to St. Paul's, I have only pleasant memories. As evidence, a recurring dream is presenting myself at 97 Beacon Street, and explaining to an astonished Mr. Greenough that I wish to re-enter his school to brush up on Latin and Greek. There was little of the teasing and none of the hazing later experienced in boarding school; they were all fine manly boys, full of energy and fun. A few years ago Ted Pickman and I found we could still recite most of our class roll — Leland, Mackay, Mason, Minot, Morison, Pickman, Shaw, Sigourney, Swift, Warren, Wigglesworth. All these boys I knew in later life, all had worthy careers.

Many years later, when as a Harvard instructor I attended an Overseers' Visiting Committee dinner, presided over by Mr. Vail, the American Telephone and Telegraph head, we were discussing preparatory schools. Mr. Vail revealed that he had been a great friend of Mr. Greenough, who bewailed the fact that "not one of his pupils could ever possibly become a scholar." I raised a laugh by pointing out that of the boys in school with me, Alfred Vincent Kidder had become a renowned anthropologist, Edward Motley Pickman a good medievalist, Edward Wigglesworth an instructor in geology and authority on cattle breeding, Richard M. Field a professor of geology at Princeton, and Dave Webster a professor of physics at Stanford. Not one of these boys studied in school the subjects which he made his life's work; but all benefited from the thorough training there in the classics and mathematics. Of course what Mr. Greenough meant was that none of his boys would become scholars in the classics, which was what one meant by "scholar" when he was young; nor did they. We had all had our fill of Latin and Greek by the time we entered college, and reached out into other fields.

Photograph by Henry Peabody, courtesy of the Society for the Preservation of New England Antiquities

Swan boats in the Public Garden, circa 1905. These unusual boats began operating in 1877, and by the early 1900s were already a city landmark.

Samuel Eliot in his library at 44 Brimmer Street in the spring of 1898.

SOCIAL LIFE

ONE CLICHÉ to which I raise no objection is "The Gay Nineties." Gay they were, for the household at 44 Brimmer Street. Grandfather and Mother always seemed to be laughing. Grandmother went about her household duties humming little ditties, and the maids sang at their work. The Morisons frequently dined out, either at friends' houses or at restaurants, such as Marliave's and Locke-Ober's. They went to weekend parties at Arthur Little's in Swampscott, or the Jacksons in Prides; they were avid theatregoers, and sang lyrics from Gilbert and Sullivan, De Koven and the like to me in the nursery; and they took part in private theatricals. My mother was gay and flirtatious; Uncle George Morison used to bring to us his bachelor friends to be entertained, and they in turn were assiduous partygivers. Two musical bachelors, Henry Goodrich and Francis H. B. Byrne, lived at No. 5 Otis Place; and William F. Apthorp, an eminent musical critic, and his beautiful wife Octavie, at No. 14. Their house was built expressly for entertainment; they had late supper parties for most of the visiting divas, actors and actresses, and always included my parents, imparting a touch of Bohemia to their social life. I remember standing on the Otis Place sidewalk late one night to see the fascinating Sarah Bernhardt alight from a cab, to attend an Apthorp party given in her honor.

As this suggests, I, too, was an avid theatregoer. So was my cousin Mac, and we generally managed to pool our resources to attend a show every Saturday. Once, dead broke when Weber and Fields came to town with Lillian Russell and De Wolfe Hopper in the cast, in desperation we persuaded my grandmother to take us. The good lady, to whom Weber and Fields had been represented as comic-opera impresarios of a high order, knew that she had been "had," but took it like a very good sport — *"Very* vulgar, but I suppose you boys just *had* to see Lillian Russell!" The Hanlon Brothers' extravaganza *Superba* we never missed on its annual visit to Boston; Maude Lessing's dark Irish beauty in *Jack and the Beanstalk* attracted our deepest devotion; Edna May in *The Belle of New York* we regarded as somewhat overrated; and of course we also were taken to see Irving and Terry in Shakespeare, and many other good plays. The Metropolitan Opera in those days held a two weeks' engagement at the enormous Boston Theatre, which ran between Mason and Washington Streets; and at an early age I heard Melba, Emma Eames, Calvé, and the De Reszkes. The Castle Square Theatre had an excellent stock company, with a weekly change of bill, and a top price of fifty cents; the Old Howard had not yet become the scene of strippers, but featured vaudeville turns which had already appeared at Keith's, with off-color jokes added. Boston even had a "ten-twenty-thirty" house of melodrama, the so-called Grand Opera House at the corner of Dover and Washington Streets, where one could hiss the villains in *Uncle Tom's Cabin, East Lynne,* and all the old standbys.

The social flavor of that period was expressed largely in dining out. People were always giving dinners or going to friends' dinners; and these affairs, from our standpoint, were characterized by an excessive amount of food; eight courses seems to have been considered the proper thing. Even with the abundant domestic staffs of that era, supplemented by "accommodators" on dinner nights, there must have been an appalling amount of planning by the lady of the house, and cooking, serving and dishwashing by the servants. Here, for instance, from my grandmother's notebook, is "Dinner for the Playfairs" on 20 October 1888. Sir Lyon (later Lord) Playfair was an eminent Scots chemist, who married as second wife Edith Russell, some thirty years his junior. She was one of the belles of the period (as her portrait by Sargent, now owned by Mason Hammond, proves) and had been virtually engaged to my Uncle Willy, for whom she always kept a tender memory.

Dinner for the Playfairs

Mr. S. H. Russell

Lady Playfair	*Mrs. S. Eliot*
Percy Lowell	*Sir Lyon Playfair*
Mrs. S. H. Russell	*Mr. Agassiz*

Mr. S. Eliot

Oysters
Brown Soup
Smelts, sauce tartare
Sweetbreads in cups
Chops broiled, macédoine
Chicken zephyre with peas
Ducks, celery & lettuce
Water ice
Sauterne, Sherry, Champagne, Burgundy

Percy Lowell was the astronomer brother of A. Lawrence Lowell, also a frequent guest at 44 Brimmer; Mr. Agassiz was Alexander Agassiz, curator of the Museum of Comparative Zoölogy at Harvard. The faculty of the University at that time was closely integrated with Boston society, and there were few dinners here where one or more professors were not present.

A "Whist Club" also figures in the family records. Apparently, the members gave parties at home, with prizes, but asked numerous nonmembers in as well, and the card playing was followed by a hot supper, with oysters, game, ice cream and champagne.

On 21 April 1890, the Eliots gave a "Musical Afternoon" from four-thirty to six, at which "Mrs. Julia L. Wyman of Chicago sang six songs for $50." Mr. Ethelbert W. Nevin (composer of "Narcissus" and "The Rosary") accompanied her on the piano for the modest fee of $25. Over forty local guests attended, as well as the Ladenburgs from New York and the Robert Morisons from Baltimore. Music, apparently, was not supposed to create an appetite, like Whist; as the only refreshments were tea, chocolate and cake.

Four eight-course dinners were given in the same household between 2 January and 3 February, 1891. One January day of 1894, six-year-old me got into the entertainment record with "Sammy's party," but there was "a dreadful snowstorm and only four came, though eight accepted." The four were my schoolmates Francis Yeats-Brown and Amos Chapman, and the Eliot twins, Sam and Molly. The glass tree, with glass baskets hanging from the branches, which had been miraculously preserved unbroken since the eighteenth cen-

SOCIAL LIFE 51

tury, was on the table; the refreshments were "pink and white ice cream," cake, milk, and sandwiches. But this party, for want of attendance, must have been rather a flop.

In addition to these entertainments for both sexes and all ages, both Grandfather and Father were members of those typically Boston institutions which had been going on since colonial days, dining clubs. The Harvard Class of 1839 celebrated both its fortieth and fiftieth reunions by a dinner at 44 Brimmer Street. "John's Club Dinner" on 2 March 1894 provided a menu which makes me wonder how people of that generation could stow away so many calories:

Oysters, radishes
Clear Soup
Roe Shad, cucumbers
Creamed Chicken, string beans
Filet beef, brussels sprouts, mushrooms
Roman punch
Four Ducks, salad of celery & lettuce
Cheese and olives
Ice cream
Coffee

Wines

*Liebfraumilch, Sherry (Manzanilla), Champagne
(Ruinart Brut, and Cordon Rouge), Burgundy
(Pommard); Cordials, Chartreuse*

Grandmother also went in for patriotic societies, such as the Colonial Dames, and the D.A.R. (then in its innocent heyday); and for these she took a great deal of teasing in the family. All records of food consumption at parties were

broken at a lunch for the Warren & Prescott Chapter, D.A.R.,
on 27 April 1895. Seventy-five ladies sat down to a repast that
included turkey salad, chartreuse of grouse, creamed oysters,
lobster farci, fourteen dozen sandwiches, and three and a
half gallons of ice cream and water ice. Grandmother adds
to her notes: "Had one extra cook. Two extra waitresses, two
women to clean up, two men to move furniture, two car-
penters to take off the doors, three dozen folding chairs."
Grandfather, who always "groaned" over these big parties,
complained that on this occasion he was run out of his own
home, and had to spend the day at the Athenaeum. The
"Daughters" must have gone home breathing hard and eager
for a chance to shed their corsets. No wonder that they
elected my grandmother their Regent, and that my mother
succeeded to it after her death.

Although we always attended the immense Christmas Tree
celebration at Trinity Church, we also held our own. In
1895 it was attended by four Amory Eliot children (Lydia,
Sam, Molly and Rosamond), three Robbinses (Elise, Juliet and
Blake), Griswold and Davenport Hayward, Bill Wendell,
Annie Nelson, Isabel, Leslie and MacGregor Morison,
Alice Thorndike, Curtis Parker, and a few grownups. All
these children, except one, of whom I have lost sight, remained my friends through life, which for some did not last
long. Curtis Parker, genial classmate and good sailor, died
when in college; Blake Robbins, in World War I, and
"Davvy" Hayward, the organizer of yacht racing at Northeast
Harbor, shortly after. Bill Wendell is still going strong; and
Lydia Eliot, now Mrs. Quincy Shaw, is a living illustration
of Shakespeare's lines:

Age cannot wither her, nor custom stale
Her infinite variety . . .

Much of the entertaining here was for friends from other cities, or people from elsewhere who were staying with friends in Boston. On 24 March 1896, "Mrs. Robinson of Virginia and her daughter-in-law, Mrs. Wait Robinson of Cambridge" are given a dinner party, with Rector Peabody of Groton, the George Shattucks, Robert Treat Paines and De Forest Danielsons among the guests. On 15 December there was a small dinner, to which my mother wrote the enigmatic note, "This dinner nearly prostrated the family, owing to the combination of Mr. Fitzgerald and Mr. Wadsworth." The first, probably, was James Fitzgerald, a very "haw-haw" Englishman who married Lady Playfair's sister; and the second, Austin Wadsworth of Geneseo, New York, whose family kept the old Harrison Gray Otis house on Beacon Street as a town residence. I imagine that the two fell out over discussing Grover Cleveland's foreign policy.

A very welcome house guest was Elizabeth Hopkins, an exceptionally beautiful young lady from Baltimore. While at our house she was "rushed" by the most eligible of Boston's bachelors, Percival Lowell the astronomer. Percy wished to take Miss Hopkins to view Bunker Hill Monument and my parents consented, provided I — aged about ten — went along as chaperon. We three drove in a hack to Charlestown, alighted near the base of the monument; and there, to Percy's disgust and my delight, were two other smitten bachelors, each bearing a large bouquet of flowers and eager to help Miss Hopkins climb the monument. So we were quite a party that day. But it is sad to record that Miss Hopkins rejected all her Boston suitors and married a Baltimorean.

Owing, probably, to the fact that one of my great-aunts married Commodore Horatio Bridge USN, my grandparents always cultivated the successive commandants of the First Naval District. I well recall a visit with my grandmother to Admiral and Mrs. Sampson at the Charlestown Navy Yard, in the fall of 1899, because the Admiral sent me on board the old receiving ship U.S.S. *Wabash,* to be measured by the naval tailor for a sailor suit, complete with bell-bottomed trousers. And in the notebook for 19 February 1900 is a dinner for Captain and Mrs. Joseph Gale Eaton USN, including General and Mrs. Charles Greely Loring, the Richard Henry Danas, and the Amory Eliots. The Captain and lady were certainly well fed, with the usual eight courses. Sherry, sauterne, claret, and champagne accompanied the appropriate courses; and I doubt not that when the "fizz" came on my father offered a toast to "The United States Navy," unsuspecting that little Sammy (who made surreptitious descents on the pantry to have a whack at the ice cream) would one day be said Navy's historian.

While the principal vehicle of social life was the small dinner, there were also tea parties or receptions. Cocktail parties were unheard of; cocktails and whiskey were considered a men's club or barroom drink, and I never saw a cocktail served in a private house (and that a very weak one, mostly vermouth) until around 1910. There were also debutante balls, to which older people were invited more often than now; and subscription assemblies, managed by the elegant Samuel Hooper Hooper. Until the Somerset Hotel was built, balls and assemblies were generally held in Mechanics Hall, now torn down to make way for the Prudential Center. Mechanics Hall was also used for indoor track meets, food fairs, dog shows, cat shows, and the like. The last ball ever given there — a very "posh" one, with ices brought from Philadelphia and terrapin from Baltimore — was held so soon after the annual dog show that a strong odor of canines and sawdust overcame the perfume that the ladies brought in.

The dance hit of the year around 1892 was inadvertently furnished by one of the Beebe brothers. This pair of bachelors attended every party, stalking about with crushed opera hats under their arms, as one sees in the old Du Maurier cartoons in *Punch*. They never danced, and usually drank too much. This particular party was a housewarming at Dedham, first of our fashionable suburbs beyond Brookline and Chestnut Hill. The couple who gave it, not intending to keep horses, made over the previous owner's carriage house for dancing. Unfortunately they neglected to do anything to the adjoining coachman's W.C., a very old-fashioned one with a wooden seat that had lost its hinges. One of the Beebes, after drinking deep, resorted to this doubtful *retrete*, whence he emerged, carrying under his arm, instead of his opera hat, the wooden seat.

In addition to dinners and other entertainments there was a constant exchange of calls. At the beginning of every winter season, Grandmother sent out cards to some two hundred families, announcing that she and my mother would be "at home" on, say, the second Thursday of each month. On these occasions they dispensed tea to anywhere from twenty to fifty callers who dropped in between three and six. Twice

or thrice a week they drove about the Back Bay, leaving cards
on some families, and calling on others. I was persuaded to
go Sunday calling with my grandmother, in the usual hired
hack, a few weeks before she died. As we drove up Beacon
Street, down Marlborough, and up Commonwealth, mostly
to slip in visiting cards, but at three or four houses to con-
sume a buffuous tea, I amused myself asking my grandmother
who lived in each house. She knew just about half of them.

These calls were by no means restricted to ladies; the more
sociable husbands and "eligible bachelors" also attended.
Sunday afternoon was the time for Harvard upperclassmen to
make their party calls. One could see them, resplendent in
frock coat, fancy waistcoat and high hat, carrying a cane,
walking up and down Commonwealth Avenue to call on the
mammas who had invited them to dine or dance. And woe
betide them if they failed to turn up within a week or two
— they were struck off "the list."

Besides all this mixed society, the ladies had their sewing
circles (which meant having a big lunch at each other's
houses, and then sewing garments for the poor), and the
gentlemen had their clubs, which made no pretense of doing
anything for the poor. In the nineties, Boston had most of
the leading clubs that are still going today — the Somerset,
Union, Union Boat, St. Botolph, University, Tavern, Algon-
quin and Country. Several others, such as the downtown Exchange, the Puritan on the corner of Beacon and Spruce
Streets, and the Boston Athletic Association, have since been
given up. Members spent much more time in their clubs
than they do now. Few gentlemen came directly home from
downtown offices; they dropped in at a club for a game of

poker, a chat, and a drink; and if entertainment at home was considered inadequate, the head of the house slipped out for more of the same between dinner and bedtime.

Small boys were required, most unwillingly on their part, to attend dancing school. My first was held at the George von Lengerke Meyer house, No. 55 Beacon Street. There I met the fascinating Meyer daughters, dark Julia and blond Alice with the big blue eyes. They evidently made a greater impression on me than I on them; for when my Priscilla met the elder — Donna Julia Brambilla — at Washington a few years ago, she remarked bluntly, "Sammy seems to have turned out pretty well. He used to be a horrid, pimply little boy, and we never thought he would amount to anything!"

Ah, those pimples! They were the great cross of my young life. I tried dosing them with lotions, prescribed by the famous Doctor "Skinny" White. I exercised regularly and vigorously. I even cut out the daily ice-cream soda and candy. Nothing worked, except, finally, just growing up.

This account of dinners and the like may sound stuffy, but the dinners themselves, judging by the talk and laughter which floated upstairs, were very gay. And there was plenty of social life outside dinners and dances. One form of enjoyment at that period was amateur theatricals, and several of the amateur theatre groups then organized, such as the Footlight Club and the Concord Players, still survive. A variant to theatricals, which had the advantage of requiring less rehearsing, was *Mrs. Jarley's Waxworks*. The players dressed up as costumed wax models of various historical or literary characters, and were carried onto the stage. "Mrs. Jarley," the mistress of ceremonies, went to each one, made a few pointed remarks which generally contained witticisms about the actors as well, and held up a clockwork box to the back of the figure, which she pretended to wind up. The figures then went stiffly through the expected evolution: Sir Walter Raleigh (Arthur Little) spread his cloak for Queen Elizabeth (my mother), and the like. This particular group of wax-works, partly owing to the wit of the M.C., Mrs. William F. Apthorp, was so successful that the members remained friends for life, and called one another by their stage names — Ernest Jackson, for instance, was "Ajax," and Nellie Eldridge, "Fair Rosamond." The picnic party on a stranded yacht, shown in one of our illustrations, was a "Waxworks" reunion.

This ephemeral group has even left its mark on a Boston street. Arthur Little, one of the foremost architects of that era, built a new house on a little street running off Bay State Road, and so was allowed by the city to name the street. He named it Raleigh Street, and his house, No. 2, which for many years remained the outermost house on Bay State Road, is still there.

Picnic party at Loring Beach, Pride's, about 1888. *Left to right on the port side:* Anna Jackson, John H. Morison, Ernest Jackson. *Starboard side:* Emily Morison, Arthur D. Little, Caleb W. Loring, Nellie Eldridge. Mr. Loring owned the boat *Lily,* wrecked on the beach.

Retreating from the hot city at Fort Independence, Pleasure Bay, South Boston, circa 1905.

The Eliot sisters—Molly, Lydia, and Rosamond.

THOSE ALLEGED PREJUDICES

WHAT OF opinions and prejudices, political and social? There I have a bone to pick with gossip columnists and novelists masquerading as social historians. According to them, Boston society was stuffy, provincial, purse-proud, prejudiced, and one hundred per cent Republican. So far as my observations go, it was none of these. My grandfather and father were independents, then known as "mugwumps." The first mention I remember of politics was Grandfather talking with marketmen, bewailing the fact that McKinley instead of Thomas B. Reed won the Republican nomination for President in 1896. Grover Cleveland was regarded as the best President since Abraham Lincoln; and we all knew by heart this ditty, to help memorize the names of the Presidents:

> WASHINGTON *first of the Presidents stands,*
> *Next placid John Adams attention commands;*
> *Thomas Jefferson's third on the glorious score,*
> *And square Jimmy Madison comes number four.*
> *Fifth on the list is plain James Monroe,*
> *And John Quincy Adams is sixth — don't you know?*
> *After Jackson comes Martin Van Buren, true blue,*
> *Then Harrison, hero of Tippecanoe.*
> *Then Tyler, the first of the Vice's to rise;*

> *Then Polk, and then Taylor, the second who dies.*
> *Then Fillmore, a Vice, takes the President's place*
> *And small Franklin Pierce is fourteenth in the race.*
> *Fifteenth is Buchanan; and following him*
> *The great name of* LINCOLN *makes all others dim.*
> *After Johnson comes Grant, with the laurel and bays,*
> *And following him is one Rutherford Hayes.*
> *Then Garfield, then Arthur, then Cleveland the fat;*
> *Then Harrison wearing his grand-daddy's hat.*
> *Adroit little Ben, twenty-third in the train;*
> *And following him, the bold* CLEVELAND *again.*

My father, a member of the Civil Service Reform Association and the Tariff Reform League, and a contributor to Godkin's New York *Nation,* ran for the City Council in 1892 as a Democrat, and for representative in the General Court four lears later, as an Independent. His candidacy, in the latter instance, was endorsed by such men as Major Henry L. Higginson, William Minot, and Dr. Maurice H. Richardson, the celebrated surgeon. The *Boston Evening Transcript* even promoted him in an editorial. In both contests he was defeated; in the latter by the regular Republican candidate, a Negro. This did not, however, create any race prejudice in the 44 Brimmer Street household.

My description of the social life may have created the impression that our family at 44 Brimmer lived only for calls and parties. That would not be correct. Grandfather worked many hours at his desk on the affairs of the Massachusetts General Hospital, the McLean Hospital, the Perkins Institute for the Blind, and other major charities of which he was director or chairman of the board; and he often visited them, sometimes with little me in tow. It was thus that I met the remarkable Helen Keller. The Boston Public School

Association, which for many years did keep the schools out of politics, was organized in our library. My grandmother and mother were particularly interested in the Society for the Prevention of Cruelty to Children. My father and mother frequently attended hearings at the State House to support or oppose some pending bill. One which they vigorously advocated was a bill to prevent the taking out of life insurance on very young children. Workers of the S.P.C.C. found that insurance agents were working over the slums, persuading parents to take out policies on babes and sucklings for a few cents a day; the prize being that if the poor child died the insurance would pay for a swell funeral. In effect, children were being denied food so that they could be buried in style. I well remember my parents' indignation over this state of affairs, and their scornful imitation of a prominent Republican politician, a friend of theirs too, who defended the insurance company: "No-body would be so croo-el as to deny food to a little che-ild!"

Nor was there, among Bostonians we knew, any of the snobbish eighteenth century despising of "trade," which persisted, though in an attenuated form, in other cities. Most of the families we knew were professional people or bankers, but many were not, and almost everyone, including the Eliots and Otises, had mercantile ancestors, whose advertisements you could read in the old *Columbian Centinel.* Aunt Leslie Morison, one of Boston's great ladies, was the daughter of a wholesale grocer, and it was observed with tolerant amusement that her son Mac, my pal, started a little "store" in a room of their Commonwealth Avenue house, where he made a tidy profit selling spools of thread and similar household requirements to his mother and her friends, at a mark-up of one cent. Boston's most famous lady, Mrs. Jack Gardner, derived the fortune that built Fenway Court from Stewart's department store in New York. Here I may cite an exception that provoked general mirth. At the Museum of Fine Arts may now be seen the portrait by John Singleton Copley of Paul Revere at his workbench, making one of those silver teapots for which he became famous before he took to dispatch riding for the Sons of Liberty. The Revere family of Canton, who owned this portrait, were ashamed of it "because it showed Mr. Revere in his shirtsleeves, like a common workman," kept it in the attic, and allowed it to be exhibited but once in the last century.

Within the Boston society in which I grew up there were no distinctions of wealth. We were vaguely conscious our families were "top drawer," although there was not yet any Social Register to tell us so. Once you were "in," more or less wealth made no difference. Captain John Bigelow USA, and his beautiful wife, who was Mary Dallam of Baltimore, came to Boston in 1894, he having been assigned by the Army to teach at M.I.T. They had nothing but army pay to live on, and dwelt in a modest wooden house near Coolidge Corner, but they went everywhere, although unable to "pay back" with anything more than good conversation and charm; and their children, who went to public school, were among my best friends. It was not until I went to St. Paul's School, then favored by Pittsburgh and New York millionaires, that I encountered the notion that one's social rating depended on such externals as steam yachts, stables of race horses and Newport "cottages." It is true that Boston society was too simple to attract bloated "gate-crashers"; nor did it breed multi-millionaires. People such as they stormed the social citadels of New York, Washington, Newport and London.

Social status, which, according to Vance Packard, every American seeks to win (or, if he has it, to keep) did not trouble us or our friends for a moment. New families were being accepted every year. The way to get in was to buy a town house on Commonwealth Avenue or Beacon Street, and a place on the North Shore, and send your children to private schools in the Back Bay. A certain minimum of breeding and manners was required, and that minimum, I believe, was much higher than in New York; possibly lower than in Philadelphia or Baltimore. Ancestry did not count in the least. Many families of ancient lineage dropped out of society simply because they did not care to incur the expense and trouble incident on dining out constantly. I remember my mother saying of one rather mousy little lady, "Poor Mary, she wouldn't make an effort, so now nobody calls on her." And there was no social institution in Boston like the Philadelphia Assembly or the Baltimore Bachelors' Cotillion, to which one simply *had* to belong to be "in." The Boston Assembly, a take-it-or-leave-it affair, was given up after World War I.

Bostonians, according to the novelists, were supposed to be highly race-conscious, bigoted Protestants, nasty to the Irish. I never heard any of that. Both sides of my family were proud of their Irish blood; the Morisons had a transmitted story of the 1689 Siege of Londonderry, in which their first American ancestor spent hours watching a rathole in the hope of catching his dinner. George Duncan, ancestor of the

Eliots, was one of the founders of the Charitable Irish Society. In close daily contact as we were with Irish maids and workmen, we could believe no ill of the Irish; and my grandmother, after visiting friends in Ireland, used to tell everyone, "The Irish gentleman is the world's finest gentleman." The family was, to be sure, down on corrupt Irish politicians, but it was down on corruption of any kind, by no matter whom. The one man whose name (as I remember) aroused their anger and contempt was General Benjamin F. Butler, that "hero" of New Orleans and Bermuda Hundred. A hardy perennial bill offered in the General Court was to provide an equestrian statue of General Butler in the State House grounds. It was first promoted by William L. Reed, the Negro who defeated my father; and later by Martin Lomasney, boss of old Ward 8. Grandfather used to say that if ever a statue were erected to "that rascal Butler" in the State House grounds, he would sell 44 Brimmer Street and move out of the Commonwealth.

There are fashions in churches, as in everything else; and it was rumored that ambitious ladies from the outer periphery joined the "right" church in order to meet the "right" people. The Anglo-Catholic Church of the Advent, on the corner of Mt. Vernon and Brimmer Streets north of our house, was not at all fashionable; but I should hate to think that my parents and grandparents left it for that reason. Phillips Brooks (I can just remember seeing Bishop Brooks, as he then was, on the street, a majestic figure in frock coat, white tie and top hat) was probably responsible for their being drawn to Trinity Church; he was not only a personal friend, but the most eloquent and inspiring preacher Boston has ever heard. The Church of the Advent, in my childhood, had as rector the rather severe, ascetic Dr. Frisbie. Services at Trinity, in those days, were decidedly "low"; there was no altar, only a communion table, no vested choir of boys and men, but an adult quartet who occupied the gallery at the west end, behind the congregation. Since I was not interested in sermons, it was a treat for me occasionally to be taken by my mother to the Church of the Advent, where one had the beauty of the traditional ritual, and superlatively good music.

Friendships, however, were not sectarian; most of our friends were Unitarian, and attended King's Chapel or the Arlington Street Church or the First Church in Boston. All the Eliots except my grandparents were Unitarians. King's Chapel was a peculiar compromise worked out by conscientious New Englanders who couldn't take the doctrine of the Trinity, yet yearned for beauty and tradition in worship. So they got up a special edition of the Book of Common Prayer, with references to the Trinity and the Divinity of Jesus deleted. A traveling Englishman who strayed into King's Chapel one Sunday shortly after met President Eliot, and complained that the service seemed "expurgated," to which "Prexy" retorted severely, "Not expurgated, *washed*."

The brick church designed by Asher Benjamin and built in 1807, at the corner of Charles and Mt. Vernon Streets, has passed through the hands of a number of sects. During my childhood it was African Methodist, serving the respectable colored community that lived on the northern slope of Beacon Hill. After most of the West End Negroes moved to Roxbury — a change they must have regretted — the Charles Street meeting house became for a time a community church, and is now Universalist. When I asked Grandfather to tell me the difference between Unitarians and Universalists, he replied, "The Universalists believe that God is too good to damn anyone, but the Unitarians believe they are too good for God to damn!"

A branch of the Otis family were Roman Catholics, and we respected that ancient faith even though we did not embrace it. The only thing I even heard of the American Protective Association, the "A.P.A." which tried to revive the anti-Catholic Know-Nothingism of the 1850's, was a ditty we used to sing:

> *Where is the mick that threw the brick?*
> *He'll never throw another —*
> *For calling me an A.P.A.*
> *He now is under cover!*

As for anti-Semitism, I never even heard of it. My father died before the furore about Louis D. Brandeis's appointment to the Supreme Court; but I expect he would have approved, as he admired Brandeis professionally, and as our neighbor at 4 Otis Place, we often talked with him. I do not believe that our family was exceptionally liberal. If they had been regarded as mavericks, a small boy would certainly have heard thereof in a disagreeable way. It was simply that nineteenth century liberalism, an atmosphere of live and let live, was the climate of opinion in that time and place.

Another favorite cliché of latter-day gossip columnists is that Boston society was fanatically pro-British, aped the English aristocracy, and all that. My recollections are all to the contrary; and one of my boyhood friends from New York, a girl who married a Bostonian, told me that the one thing that struck her on coming here was that Boston was still fighting the War of Independence. The traditions of the American Revolution were central to my upbringing; memorials and landmarks of it were all about us. Popular extra-curricular reading was Charles Carleton Coffin's *Boys of '76* — Philip Weld told me that I must read it, or fight him! I was proud of Faneuil Hall and the Adamses, highly approved the Cleveland-Olney diplomatic sock-in-the-jaw to Lord Salisbury, firmly believed America to be the best country and Boston the finest city on earth; and that the United States Navy, having "licked England twice," could do so again, if necessary. It was only after growing up that I began to entertain feelings of kindness and admiration toward our mother country.

Boston society certainly was provincial in some respects — what society of a non-metropolitan city is not? But it was worldly too. Almost every family we knew had connections abroad, and in other parts of the United States. My mother, as a girl of seventeen, was taken to Germany by the William F. Apthorps, who were well known there in musical circles; she heard the *Ring* at Bayreuth, met Frau Cosima Wagner and Franz Liszt. My grandparents were then staying at the Château de Rabodanges in Normany, which belonged to a French gentleman who had married an Otis. They had just been entertained by the Playfairs and Sir Richard Temple in London, and might well have continued to Florence, where they had friends among the American artistic community described by Van Wyck Brooks in *The Dream of Arcadia*. It was the same in the United States. Hospitable houses were open to us in New York, Philadelphia, Baltimore and Washington; and when I first visited the far west in 1904, I was passed on from one family friend or cousin to another in Arizona and California.

Someone explaining the decay of American cities since 1940 observed that we had no solid core of nobility and bourgeois, as in Amsterdam, Strasbourg, Bordeaux, Bristol, and Milan, who insisted on living in town, interested themselves in local politics and supported cultural activities. But Boston had just that sort of group in my childhood. Not nobility, of course, but families who endowed Harvard and other universities, founded the Museum of Fine Arts, the Symphony Orchestra and the Opera House, and took pride in supporting great charitable foundations such as the Perkins Institute for the Blind and the Massachusetts General Hospital. And Boston had something more than that. Despite all the sneers and jeers at "Proper Bostonians," "Boston Brahmins" and the like, there was a remarkable pattern of living here that existed nowhere else in the United States. When a family had accumulated a certain fortune, instead of trying to build it up still further to become a Rockefeller or Carnegie or Huntington and then perhaps discharge its debt to society by some great foundation, it would step out of business or finance and try to accomplish something in literature, education, medical research, the arts, or public service. Generally one or two members of the family continued in business, to look after the family securities and enable the creative brothers or cousins to carry on without the handicap of poverty. Of course there were families like that in other cities, but in Boston there were so many of them as to constitute a recognized way of life. One only has to think of the Prescott, Parkman, Shattuck, Cabot, Holmes, Lowell, Forbes, Peabody, Eliot, Saltonstall and Sargent families and what they have accomplished for the beauty and betterment of life, to see what I mean.

For this atmosphere I am deeply grateful, for it was never suggested that "Sammy" should go into business, or make money, or do anything but what his tastes and talents impelled him to do, no matter how unremunerative. By way of contrast, my best friend at St. Paul's School was a New Yorker, who went to Yale. He had a nice talent for writing — made *Yale Lit.* in college — and also at painting; and he had far more wealth behind him than I. But, when we talked over life on summer cruises, and I outlined what I hoped to accomplish with the pen, he shook his head sadly over my urgings that he become a writer or an artist. It was expected of him, he said rather wistfully, that he go on the New York Stock Exchange in order to keep his family's financial standing at a high level. He did just that, and has had a pretty miserable time in so doing.

11

A FEW CELEBRITIES

TWO WELL-KNOWN Boston international marriages come off very well in Hesketh Pearson's recent book *The Marrying Americans,* since both were love matches, not merely exchanges of titles for dollars. Of one, the idyllic though brief union of Edward Twistleton and Ellen Dwight, we heard a good deal from Ellen's niece Mrs. William W. Vaughan, the mother of my pal Sam. Mary Endicott, who married Joseph Chamberlain, I even knew later when, after Joe's death, she had married Canon Carnegie. She was a brilliant, highly intelligent lady, who tried without much success to drive a little common sense on international matters into her stepson Neville Chamberlain.

If only someone would now write a book on the *non*-marrying Americans, the gay ladies who had amorous overseas adventures with potentates and princes! Of one — her first name Fanny is all I can now recall — I read in one of the Edwardian memoirs that came out early in this century, and mentioned her to my mother. It certainly rang a bell with her. Fanny, who was on the fringe of Boston society, but whose family declined to furnish her with funds commensurate to her beauty, charm and natural soprano voice, used to encourage the Boston beaux of the period to take her out walking. She would guide them to Hovey's on Summer Street, or some other shop favored by the social elect, make purchases, discover that she had no money with her, ask her swain to pay for them, either by money or check; of course Papa would repay him next day. Papa never did; and Fanny never paid for these favors with anything more substantial than a kiss on the doorstep at the close of an expensive outing. Eventually, after the word had got around, Fanny decided that London was a better theatre for her talents. By some means or other she raised the steamer fare, and on board ship met a rich Englishman who set her up with a house, servants and expense account in Mayfair. There she became a celebrity in the set that revolved around the Prince of Wales, and incidentally became one of his mistresses, a rival to Mrs. Langtry, "The Jersey Lily." My mother recalled that one of the Otis ladies called on Fanny in London and was invited to one of her song recitals. When she related this on her return, one of her friends remonstrated, "How could you call on that awful woman?" To which Miss Otis gallantly replied, "I shall never believe a word against Fanny's reputation — she has such a lovely singing voice!" — surely a non-sequitur if there ever was one.

A Bostonian who knew almost everyone in the top political world of nineteenth century England was Dr. William Everett, son of Edward Everett. "Piggy" Everett, as he was nicknamed in Boston because of his slovenly dress and somewhat disgusting personal habits, attended Trinity College, Cambridge, when his father was American minister to the Court of St. James's. At Trinity, one of his fellow students was Fanny's future lover, the Prince of Wales. They never corresponded; but when Piggy visited London in 1902, and his former pupil, the Honorable Joseph Choate, was American ambassador, he decided to call on King Edward. Dr. Everett walked into the embassy on Grosvenor Street, demanding of an astonished clerk that he send a note around to Buckingham Palace. The clerk, taking him for a shabby eccentric, demurred. He then insisted that his card be sent up to the Ambassador. Presently Joe Choate himself came bouncing down the stairs, both hands extended, ordering the clerks to do anything that his "dear old friend Dr. Everett" wanted. The note was duly dispatched by messenger, and Piggy sat down to wait, the clerks and secretaries exchanging winks and wondering how they would ever get rid of him. Half an hour later a royal brougham drove up, and the footman, alighting, presented Dr. Everett with a note which he proceeded to open and read aloud to the astonished embassy staff. It went something like this:

> *My dear Everett,*
> *You have shamefully neglected me all these years. Come at once to the Palace, and we will talk over old times.*
>
> > *Faithfully yours,*
> > EDWARD R. & I.

Dr. Everett leaped into the brougham, and in due course was ushered into the royal study. What they talked about I do not know; but, as an instance of the King's remarkable memory, Piggy related that Edward, having helped himself to a long Havana cigar from a box on the table, did not present one to his guest, saying "I'm not offering one to you,

Everett, for I well remember how down you were on smoking at Trinity." Down on it he always was; when I met Piggy staying at Beverly with the Lorings — the only people who would still put up with him — we were forbidden to smoke in his presence, to save us from being the object of one of his tantrums.

My father, who attended Adams Academy, Quincy, when Dr. Everett was headmaster, used to tell of one of these tantrums. A stupid boy in the Virgil class, reciting Latin, insisted, despite frequent correction, on pronouncing the name of the hero of the Aeneid as "Eé-ne-as." Finally Piggy could stand it no longer. He jumped up and down, banging the desk with his fists, exclaiming, "You goddam little fool, do you suppose that Dido would have fallen in love with a man who accented his name on the antepenult when the penult was long?"

During my boyhood the New England literary galaxy was flickering to a close. So, not counting poor Piggy, who despite great literary promise had a career *manqué,* I met but one of the great figures — Dr. Holmes. My grandfather took me to call on him, in the Beverly Farms house where his son the Justice later summered, about the year 1892. The Autocrat was in good form. Tendering what appeared to be a potted plant, he said, "Pull it up by the roots, m'lad, don't be afraid." I complied, and the fake plant came up, disclosing a hollow flowerpot containing a few chocolates wrapped in silver foil. "Just enough for me!" said Dr. Holmes, teasingly; but promptly produced a box of chocolates from which I was invited to eat my fill.

I can, however, boast having seen every President of the

United States of the last sixty years, starting with McKinley. He made an official visit to Boston early in 1899, accompanied by John Hay, the distinguished Secretary of State, John D. Long, the popular Secretary of the Navy, and the highly unpopular Secretary of War, Russell A. Alger, who had been accused of feeding "embalmed beef" to our soldiers in the Spanish War. Noble and Greenough's School was let out to see the presidential cortege pass in open victorias, and our cheerleader called for "Three long *Nobles* and three times three," for the four statesmen in succession. McKinley, Hay and Long each were given a rousing cheer; Mr. Alger a very feeble one, interspersed with rude cries of "beef! beef!" Margaret Leech relates this incident in her historical biography of McKinley; she states that there was so much hooting at Alger in Boston that he was "deeply wounded," and that it led to his resignation. If we boys could have known that, how delighted we would have been!

12

BEVERLY FARMS
AND NORTHEAST HARBOR

BEVERLY FARMS was my grandparents' summer home in the 1890's. They hired the Knowlton house near the railway station, so close to the road that they named it "Roadside." A later owner has moved it well back into the field which was then an apple orchard. There was an old barn which my cousin Mac and I invested with imaginary ghosts, celebrating an annual "revel day" every June. We were mad about bicycling, and must have covered almost every dirt road of Essex County, then far more open than today: a series of farms. I remember particularly the vast sweep of apple blossom in the late spring, the great heaps of golden squash and pumpkin in the autumn, and Sunday walks with my father, Mac, and his sisters on Beverly Commons, then an open hilly pasture. In Beverly Farms my nurse introduced me to one of the new inventions, the gramophone. One was owned in the village, and the proud owner invited friends and neighbors occasionally to listen to the marvelous thing; one left a nickel or dime in a plate at the door as a token admission fee. The selections were mostly popular or sentimental songs, or skits such as the town meetin' voting to construct the new skule house outen the materials of the old skule house, but not to pull down the old skule house till the new one was built. These were recorded on soft wax-covered cylinders which had to be handled very gingerly and brushed off with a camel's-hair brush.

A noted figure at "The Farms," as the natives called it, was Mrs. Henry Whitman, who let us use the section of West Beach in front of her house. Mr. Whitman, a shadowy figure in comparison with his wife, owned a small side-wheeler steam yacht which he used for commuting to Boston. His wife was a disciple of Ruskin. She not only cherished pre-Raphaelite art and artists, but set up a little factory of stained glass near Park Square, Boston, where she designed and executed some notable works in that medium. My parents first brought me to see her when I was seven or eight years old. She had no children of her own, but her heart seemed to go out to me, and mine to her; she encouraged me to call, received me as graciously as if I had been her friends Henry James or John Jay Chapman (whom I first met there) and carried on an intellectual conversation at my level, although I neither noted nor suspected any condescension. Every Christmas she gave me something beautiful to help form my taste: a framed photograph of an old master, or a small piece of stained glass to hang against a window. I count her as my dearest friend of that generation — about halfway between those of parents and grandparents — and as one of those who encouraged me very early in the way that eventually I chose.

Moving day to Beverly Farms, in mid-May, was a great day in the 44 Brimmer Street household. For a week previous trunks had been packed, toys selected, bicycles stacked, even favorite chairs and other pieces of furniture collected. Early on the appointed day two-horse wagons of Curtis and

Croston, movers, pulled up at the front door. They drove the baggage all the way, over the Lynn marshes, through Salem and Beverly, arriving at "Roadside" in the early afternoon, while family and servants took the train; and about mid-October the process was repeated.

There is nothing to a boy like a real pal; Mac was mine at Beverly Farms. We shared the same secrets; went into spasms of laughter over our own jokes. As a sample of this adolescent wit, we were always playing the changes on a local character, Hanable by name, who let out dories and sold bait on West Beach. He became successively Hannibal, Hasdrubal, Hamilcar, Hanno, and the Noble Carthaginian, each new pseudonym dissolving us in idiotic laughter. Absurd conversations were evolved from the billboards we observed from the Boston & Maine Railroad — such as "Magee Furnaces and Ranges are the Best." "Yes, but you must shop when in Salem at Almy, Bigelow & Washburn's." "Of course, but don't forget Fletcher's Castoria — Children Cry For It," and so on, to the utter disgust of our elders.

My parents spent every July and August at the old Rockend Hotel in Northeast Harbor, Maine. It was there that I acquired my almost passionate love for the sea and for Mount Desert Island. There, too, one met children from New York, Philadelphia, Albany and Baltimore; notably the Gardiner grandchildren of Bishop William Croswell Doane, an old family friend, who had first shown my parents the beauty of that place. At Northeast Harbor Sam Vaughan was the pal. We rowed skiffs and fished for flounders together; we spent hours in a discarded upright piano box which we named the *Cimbria* after a local steamboat, striking the bells on a sec-

tion of drainpipe that passed for a smokestack, and calling all
the landings from Bangor to Bar Harbor. The great moment
came when the actual *Cimbria* passed, and returned our frantic wavings and shoutings with a real steam-whistle salute.
From these childish games we graduated to sailing North
Haven dinghies *Rena* and *Leda*. In sailing these little cat-
rigged craft I first felt the exhilaration, the peculiar, inde-
scribable delight of sea transport under sail. Luckily for us
the gasoline motor had not yet come in; we learned our sea
lore from men who had made their living from the ocean,
and who taught us how to "hand, reef and steer" in the traditional manner.

Gathering a load of hay on Boston Common, a practice that did not survive the turn of the century.

Photograph by Henry Peabody, courtesy of the Society for the Preservation of New England Antiquities

Park Street Church and Tremont Street Mall, circa 1905.

⨞ 13 ⨟

END OF AN ERA

WE WERE at Northeast Harbor during the midsummer of the Spanish-American War. Grandfather, who loved Spain and was an excellent Spanish scholar, "groaned" over the jingoism that the war brought forth, and (like his cousin Charles Eliot Norton) despaired of the Republic; but my parents had many friends in the Army and Navy, including Captain Bigelow, who was wounded at San Juan Hill. For a small boy it was a thrilling experience — seeing the Massachusetts Volunteer Regiments march away and return, reading accounts of great victories, gloating over the discomfiture and defeat of the "dons."

That autumn Grandfather Eliot died at Beverly Farms. I was with him almost to his last day, heard him murmur over and over, "I've had a blessed life — a blessed life" — as indeed he had. Of the many tributes to him, I like best that of Charles Evans the bibliographer, whom Grandfather had put on his way to a career. Evans dedicated the fourth volume of his great *American Bibliography* to "Samuel Eliot . . . who bore through life the white flower of a Christian gentleman, and died in peace and honor."

On New Year's Eve, 1900–1901, I witnessed the ceremonious ushering in of the new century from the balcony of the

State House. We owed that privileged position to friendship with a gallant figure of the closing century, Governor Roger Wolcott. The Reverend Edward Everett Hale recited the Lord's Prayer in a sonorous voice, without benefit of loudspeaker. A cannon on the Common announced midnight, and every church bell in the city pealed forth. It was a high moment of hope and glory — peace and prosperity everywhere, save in South Africa and the Philippines where the "last" wars appeared to be petering out, Bryan defeated for the second time, Victoria still on the English throne, vistas of progress looming ahead.

Dis aliter visum.

This opening year of the new century, for me, marked the transition from childhood to youth. That summer I had my first cruise, with Sam Vaughan, in an open North Haven dinghy, around Mount Desert Island. We spent the night and cooked breakfast on board, under an old tarpaulin, but stopped over at Bartletts Island to see the Lorings; it was there that Sam met his future bride, May, and I my dear friend and classmate, Gus. In the fall of 1901 I entered St. Paul's School, which opened a new way of life for me.

Skipping my years there and at Harvard College and at "Sciences Po" in Paris, I shall conclude with an incident that happened in the spring of 1910, an incident which in retrospect seems to mark the end of an era. I was then studying for the Ph.D., living in 44 Brimmer Street. James Freeman Clarke, one of our horsiest neighbors, who drove, hacked, hunted and kept ponies for his grandchildren, had a ruddy-complexioned coachman named Charles, a friend to us all. One day Charles appeared on the street, not leading a horse or driving a carriage, but at the wheel of a car. "That's the new Cadillac," he said, "with a self-starter; Mr. Clarke wouldn't buy an auto as long as you had to crank it by hand." While we were admiring the new car we heard a strange sound overhead and looked up. It was a biplane flying over the city, the first I had ever seen airborne. "Well, now I've seen everything," said Charles.

He had. The internal combustion engine turned our economy upside-down, and placed our society on a completely new basis. Life would never be the same again.

But those last years of the nineteenth century were a great time for a boy to grow up in Boston; and I retain only happy memories of an era which opened with the horsecar and the herdic, and closed with the Cadillac and the airplane.